QUALITIES OF OUR MISSIONAL GOD

Study by James Dant
Commentary by Cecil Sherman

Free downloadable Teaching Guide for this study available at

NextSunday.com/teachingguides

NextSunday Resources
6316 Peake Road
Macon, Georgia 31210-3960
1-800-747-3016
©2014 by NextSunday Resources

TABLE OF CONTENTS

Qualities of Our Missional God

Study Introduction 1

Lesson 1 The Mobility of God
Numbers 10:11-28
Study 3
Commentary 11

Lesson 2 The Reputation of God
Numbers 14:1-23
Study 21
Commentary 31

Lesson 3 The Mercy of God
Numbers 21:1-9
Study 39
Commentary 49

Lesson 4 The Promises of God
Numbers 34
Study 57
Commentary 67

HOW TO USE THIS STUDY

NextSunday Resources Adult Bible Studies are designed to help adults study Scripture seriously within the context of the larger Christian tradition and, through that process, find their faith renewed, challenged, and strengthened. We study the Scriptures because we believe they affect our current lives in important ways. Each study contains the following three components:

Study Guide

Each study guide lesson is arranged in four movements:

Reflecting recalls a contemporary story, anecdote, example, or illustration to help us anticipate the session's relevance in our lives.

Remembering provides a frame of reference for the Scriptures.

Studying is centered on giving the biblical material in-depth attention while often surrounding it with helpful insights from theology, ethics, church history, and other areas.

Understanding helps us find relevant connections between our lives and the biblical message.

What About Me? provides brief statements that help unite life issues with the meaning of the biblical text.

Commentary

Each study guide lesson is accompanied by an additional, in-depth commentary on the biblical material. Written by a different author than the study guide, each commentary gives the opportunity for learners to approach the Scripture text from a separate but complementary viewpoint.

Teaching Guide

In addition to the provided study guide and commentary, *NextSunday Resources* also provides a *free* downloadable teaching guide, available at NextSunday.com. Each teaching guide gives the teacher tools for focusing on the content of each study guide lesson through additional commentary and Bible background information. Through teacher helps and teaching options, each teaching guide also provides substance for variety and choice in the preparation of each lesson.

NextSunday
Resources

STUDY INTRODUCTION

It was July 3, 2002. I reclined in a chair on the beach of St. George Island, Florida, reading *Numbers: A Bible Commentary for Teaching and Preaching,* by Dennis Olson. I would be willing to bet I was the only person on that beach—okay, any beach—reading that wonderful book. Two college-aged students meandered between the Gulf waters and me. One glanced at the cover of my book and remarked to her friend, "You've got to be pretty bored to read a math book at the beach."

Hearing her comment, I replied, "Actually, it's not a math book. It's a Bible commentary."

"I rest my case," she retorted and walked away.

We rarely read this fourth book of the Old Testament. We use it even less frequently as a source for missions theology. Why? Maybe it's the name. Numbers is not a very exciting title. The name is derived from the Latin *Numeri,* which is a translation of the Greek title *Arithmoi* (Mariottini, 622). This title was used in the Greek translation of the Old Testament because a census is taken twice in the book—the people are numbered.

In the Hebrew Bible, however, the title of this book is *bemidbar,* which means "in the wilderness." This is much more provocative and descriptive of the book's contents. In the wilderness, the community of faith—the Israelites—encountered facets of God's character that would define and direct them for generations to come. They would come face to face with the mobility of God, the reputation of God, the mercy of God, and the promises of God. These elements of God's nature kept the mission of Israel alive. These same elements keep the mission alive in the community of faith today.

Too often we are tempted to let "numbers" drive missions. How many churches have we built? How many dollars have we raised? How many bodies have we baptized? The book of Numbers reminds us that missions is motivated by something deeper. Missions reflects the heart and nature of God. If we can just get past the math, we can see God's nature clearly in the book of Numbers. . . in the wilderness.

Claude F. Mariottini, "The Book of Numbers," *Mercer Dictionary of the Bible,* ed. Watson E. Mills et al. (Macon: Mercer University Press, 1990).

THE MOBILITY OF GOD

Numbers 10:11-28

Central Question

How does the mission of God require us to move?

Scripture

Numbers 10:11-28 In the second year, in the second month, on the twentieth day of the month, the cloud lifted from over the tabernacle of the covenant. 12 Then the Israelites set out by stages from the wilderness of Sinai, and the cloud settled down in the wilderness of Paran. 13 They set out for the first time at the command of the LORD by Moses. 14 The standard of the camp of Judah set out first, company by company, and over the whole company was Nahshon son of Amminadab. 15 Over the company of the tribe of Issachar was Nethanel son of Zuar; 16 and over the company of the tribe of Zebulun was Eliab son of Helon. 17 Then the tabernacle was taken down, and the Gershonites and the Merarites, who carried the tabernacle, set out. 18 Next the standard of the camp of Reuben set out, company by company; and over the whole company was Elizur son of Shedeur. 19 Over the company of the tribe of Simeon was Shelumiel son of Zurishaddai, 20 and over the company of the tribe of Gad was Eliasaph son of Deuel. 21 Then the Kohathites, who carried the holy things, set out; and the tabernacle was set up before their arrival. 22 Next the standard of the Ephraimite camp set out, company by company, and over the whole company was Elishama son of Ammihud. 23 Over the company of the tribe of Manasseh was Gamaliel son of Pedahzur, 24 and over the company of the tribe of Benjamin was Abidan son of Gideoni. 25 Then the standard of the camp of Dan, acting as the rear guard of all the camps, set out, company by company, and over the whole company was Ahiezer son of Ammishaddai. 26 Over the company of the tribe of Asher was Pagiel son of Ochran, 27 and over the company of the tribe of Naphtali was Ahira son of Enan. 28 This was the order of march of the Israelites, company by company, when they set out.

Reflecting

One night as a child, I overheard pieces of my parents' conversation as they sat together on our living room sofa. My reception of their conversation was about as fuzzy as the *Brady Bunch* broadcast I was watching on our nineteen-inch Zenith television with the rabbit-ear antennae. I distinctly recognized only two phrases: "this year's vacation" and "the second week of June." That was all I needed to hear.

With my fifth-grade school year and the month of May both nearing completion, I immediately began preparing for the family excursion. The year before, we had traveled from Arkansas to Oklahoma to visit family. Two years earlier we hauled floats, beach balls, and flip-flops to Pensacola, Florida. I had no idea where the old Buick was headed in June, but I wanted to be prepared.

I went to my bedroom, pulled my brown naugahyde Samsonite from the top of my closet, and started packing all the essentials. I neatly lined the bottom of my suitcase with *Archie* comics. Then, I piled in Matchbox cars, Major Matt Mason action figures, a harmonica, and a box of dominoes. My mom entered the room and inquired as to the purpose of my activity. I told her I was packing for the vacation she and dad had been discussing. I further assured her I had left plenty of room in the suitcase for shorts, shirts, socks, and other items she felt were essential.

The smile on her face and the words that followed are now forever imprinted on my memory. "We're not going anywhere during our vacation this year," she said. "Your dad is going to use the time to paint your sister's room and put a fence in the backyard. He's looking forward to you helping him. It will be lots of fun."

"But you're supposed to *go somewhere* on vacation," I protested.

"Well, this is a stay-at-home-and-work vacation," said Mom.

My parents had obviously forgotten the meaning of the word *vacation*!

I wonder if the church has forgotten the meaning of the word *missions*.

Remembering

Israel's history is a story of movement. In Genesis 12:1, God instructed Abraham, the father of the faith, "Go from your country and your kindred and your father's house to a land that I will show you." Generations later, Joseph went to Egypt and provided food amid famine. During Joseph's time in Egypt, his family traveled to Egypt for food. In Egypt they settled—for a while.

Approximately 400 years after Joseph's journey to Egypt, his multitudinous descendants were ready to move again. The family of Abraham grew into a nation—a nation of slaves.

It became Moses' mission to deliver the children of Israel from their Egyptian slavery. Moses' story is by no means stagnant; he was constantly on the move. As a baby, he moved from the comfort of his home to the bulrushes at the edge of the Nile River. Pharaoh's daughter took him from the Nile to the palace.

As a young adult, Moses' murderous defense of a Hebrew slave moved him from the palace to the land of Midian. Then the voice of the LORD, from a burning bush atop Mt. Horeb, moved Moses from Midian back to Egypt. From Egypt, Moses moved the Israelite people to Mt. Sinai, the mountain of God. It is at the foot of this mountain that we find the children of Israel in today's Scripture lesson. They are preparing to move again.

Israel's past and the heroes of Israel's past are characterized by movement. The people became a community on the march toward their promised land (Mariottini, 622). The perceptive Israelite (and the perceptive reader of their history) quickly recognized this mobility as an inherent part of the nature of God.

Studying

Moving Day, 10:11 My family recently sold our home and moved across town. We had lived in our previous house for about four years. When the last box was loaded onto the moving truck, we walked through the old home. . . and remembered.

Israel had been camped at Mt. Sinai for almost eleven months. They had arrived at Sinai on the "third new moon" after their departure from Egypt (Ex 19:1). Now they prepared to leave in the "second year, in the second month on the twentieth day" (Num 10:11). What did the Israelites do during these months at the foot of the mountain?

Usually when this story is conveyed, we primarily focus on the Israelites' reception of the Law through Moses. Moses spent much of these eleven months in the presence of God, on the mountain, receiving the Ten Commandments and other words of instruction. In fact, he was on the mountain for such extended periods of time that the Israelites often doubted his return.

The Israelites, however, were not inactive during these months. God's earliest words to them,

Nisan is the first month of the lunar-based Jewish calendar. It is the month during which Passover is celebrated, according to Exodus 12:1-11. Israel's departure from Sinai during the second month, Iyar, allowed time for the completion of their second Passover as prescribed in Numbers 9:1-14 (Dozeman, 94).

through Moses, included detailed instructions for the construction of the ark of the covenant, the tabernacle, the altar, and the priestly vestments (Ex 25–28). Each of these items was constructed to be mobile. Israel would be a worshiping nation, but they would be a worshiping nation on the move.

The Method, 10:12-28 Having constructed their instruments of worship, the Israelites began their journey to the Wilderness of Paran. It is evident that their movement was organized and regimented. Four standards, or groups, were established, and a particular tribe led each standard.

The tribe of Judah led the first standard, which included the Gershonites and Merarites, whose task was to transport the tabernacle. The tribe of Reuben led the second standard, and it included the Kohathites, who were responsible for the holy objects kept in the tabernacle. Standards three and four were led respectively by the tribes of Ephraim and Dan. The final standard, led by Dan, served as the rear guard for the traveling nation.

One can easily imagine that every tribe and every Israelite had a task to perform. This was a well-organized march. It was, however, a march into the wilderness.

According to the boundaries established by the writer of Numbers, the Israelites wandered in the Wilderness of Paran for about thirty-eight of their forty years of migration (Levine, 307). While the exact location of this wilderness is unclear, 1 Kings 11:18 describes it as a desert site between Midian and Egypt. The writer of Numbers, however, seems to extend the boundaries to encompass a portion of the northern Sinai Peninsula (Dozeman, 94-95). In earlier biblical literature, it is the battleground of a war between Abraham and five kings, as well as the homeland of Hagar and Ishmael. For the wandering Israelite, it was simply a wilderness.

> Gershonites, Merarites, and Kohathites were divisions within the priestly tribe of Levi. Those carrying the tabernacle preceded those carrying the holy objects so that the tabernacle could be erected before the holy objects arrived.

Yet the Israelites marched into the Wilderness of Paran with absolute obedience. Verse 13 assures the reader that this movement from Sinai to Paran was a result of "the command of the LORD by Moses." This simple obedience on the part of Israel must not be overlooked. In fact, this is the last time this generation of Israelites will exhibit obedience prevalently. Order and obedience characterize the first ten chapters of Numbers. In comparison, disorder, disobedience, and death dominate Numbers 11–25 (Olson, 8). For now, we must applaud the Israelites who heard the word of God and responded by willingly walking into the risky, yet potentially rewarding wilderness.

Understanding

God commands humanity to scatter; we prefer to settle. God prompts us to go; we choose to stay. God dreams of our "going to the ends of the earth"; we institutionalize.

These conflicting goals are evident throughout the biblical record. God told Adam and Eve to multiply and fill the earth, yet they were driven from the comforts of the garden. In Genesis 11, the earth's population gathered and settled at Babel and then scattered in confusion across the land. In Acts 1, Jesus instructed his disciples to be his witnesses from Jerusalem to the uttermost parts of the earth. Yet, throughout the remainder of the book of Acts, the apostles appeared to stay in Jerusalem while other individuals such as Phillip, Barnabas, Silas, and Paul spread the gospel. We tend to settle and institutionalize.

While we can argue that our generation is mobile, we must admit that our mobility has an end—settling. We move up in the company, move on to a dream job, move into a new home, and move out to the suburbs all in an effort to settle.

Often the church's apparent practice of mobility is in reality a propensity toward settling. Churches move out of "transitional areas" (which means racially and economically diverse communities) and settle in the suburbs and outskirts of our cities. Within this new context, congregations, educational programs, buildings, and budgets can be built; we can settle. Missions becomes less defined as "going" and more understood as "sending." Our logic? A strong and settled institution has more resources available to send.

Israel was not allowed to settle at Sinai. Life with God was a journey. The God of Israel takes us away from the security of home and land and country (Dozeman, 97). Baptism does not denote residency in the church, but rather prepares us for and propels us into wilderness and world. Missions is birth in the vivid mobility of God.

What About Me?

- *The church best reflects its God and its history when it is moving.* People of faith are quick to institutionalize. In the process of expanding buildings, budgets, and memberships, we often forget the world at large—the object of God's gospel affection and the ultimate goal of gospel witness.

- *Moving is always hard and risky work.* Following Jesus' baptism, he was driven into the wilderness. After the wilderness, he walked into the world. We cannot completely accomplish ministry and missions within the comfort of sanctuary walls.

- *Everyone has a job in the missions movement.* Each tribe and each Israelite contributed to the movement of the people of faith. Today, Christ calls us to be givers, prayers, builders, painters, teachers, preachers, artists, and more in the world.

Resources

Thomas B. Dozeman, "The Book of Numbers," *The New Interpreter's Bible* (Nashville: Abingdon, 1998).

Baruch A. Levine, "Numbers 1–20," *The Anchor Bible* (New York: Doubleday, 1993).

Claude F. Mariottini, "The Book of Numbers," *Mercer Dictionary of the Bible*, ed. Watson E. Mills et al. (Macon: Mercer University Press, 1990).

Dennis T. Olson, *Numbers*, Interpretation: A Bible Commentary for Teaching and Preaching (Louisville: John Knox Press, 1996).

Walter Riggans, *Numbers*, The Daily Study Bible Series (Louisville: Westminster John Knox Press, 1983).

THE MOBILITY OF GOD

Numbers 10:11-28

Introduction

Four lessons from Numbers is a trip to the attic; most of us have not been up there in a long time. I had to do some reading about the book before I could approach the text, and I suspect most of you are in the same place I am. I've had a "crash course" in Numbers the past three days. Here are some things I learned:

1. The book gets its name from "the numbering or census of the people related in chs. 1–4 and again in ch. 26" (*The New Oxford Annotated Bible* [New York: Oxford University Press, 1991], 163 OT section). This is an unfortunate name for the text.

2. The Hebrew Bible gives the book a name that fits. They call it "In the Wilderness." In an almost random way the book tells some of the things that happened to the Hebrews in their forty years "in the wilderness."

3. Here is one outline of the book:
   A. Part I, Sinai: 1:1–12:16. Our text comes from this part (10:11-28); it describes the march from Sinai to Paran. These chapters take but nineteen days.
   B. Part II, Paran: 13:1–22:1. This part covers about thirty-eight years. No attempt is made to be either chronological or comprehensive.
   C. Part III, Moab: 22:2–36:13. These chapters are the end times for Hebrew wanderings. Soon they would cross the Jordan and enter the promised land. Time covered in this period is five to six months.

4. Moses did not write these words. He wrote things that were sources for the people who did (see 33:2). John Marsh called Numbers "a priestly reinterpretation of the history to enable Israel to see plainly her divine origin, destiny and call"

(*The Interpreter's Bible*, vol. 2 [New York: Abingdon Press, 1953], 137).

5. Numbers did not reach final form until after Babylon and exile (about 450 BC). The people who struggled in an impoverished Judah needed to get in touch with their past, and they needed reassurance for their future. Numbers gives both.

6. There is a primitive quality in parts of the text. Yahweh is Israel's god; Chemosh is Moab's god. Yahweh comes near in the tabernacle; Yahweh is awesome and frightening. No one would dare go near the tabernacle or touch the ark of the covenant. Numbers gives us clues as to the way Levites and priests came to rival Moses in leadership.

7. The strong idea in Numbers is wrapped in these three points:
   A. God is revealed in history. Numbers is not what people thought about God; it is about what God did.
   B. God wants obedience to a set of righteous laws. Theology apart from ethics is not in the book.
   C. God was able to get the Israelites through the wilderness and into the promised land—in spite of their rebellious spirit and faltering ways.

Keep these ideas in mind as we work through these studies. A word of warning: This is not a study in ancient Hebrew history. This is a Bible study in the twenty-first century. I will do some exegetical work, but I am mainly concerned with what this means to us.

The Idea That God Stayed in One Place

Ancients believed gods staked out the map. Yahweh God lived at the "holy mountain" called Horeb or Sinai. When God spoke to Moses from the "burning bush," Moses was "beyond the wilderness, and came to Horeb, the mountain of God. There the angel of the LORD appeared to him" (Ex 3:1-2). The initial request made to the "king of Egypt" was, "The LORD, the God of the Hebrews, has met with us; let us now go a three days' journey into the wilderness, so that we may sacrifice to the LORD our God" (Ex 3:18b). The point of it all was to get the Hebrews out of Egypt and to a place where Yahweh God lived. So Moses took the

Hebrews to Sinai out from under the sway of Egyptian religion and into the land where their God lived. They would linger at the "holy mountain" for eleven months. During that time they would receive the Ten Commandments and make sacred covenant with God (see Ex 19–20).

Our text describes the first move away from the "holy mountain." Are they going to go out from the presence and power of Yahweh God when they leave the holy mountain? Sounds pretty primitive, doesn't it? But let me offer you two illustrations that may make this idea come closer home.

- The girl is a freshman in college. All her life she lived in her hometown with her parents. They took her to church every Sunday. She was "at home" in that small-town congregation. Then she went to college. The church near her dorm has the same name as her home church, but it is not the same. The whole experience is different; she doesn't find God there. God is at the church back home. If some understanding soul does not intervene, this girl will drop out of church while in college. Unwittingly, she has a "place God."

- I pastored the First Baptist Church of Chamblee, Georgia, from 1956 to 1960. Atlanta was booming. Chamblee went from a small town with dairy farms to a suburb of a large city. One of my jobs was to call on people who had just moved to the city and persuade them to join my church. It was good work; sometimes it was hard work. Too often they had a "place God." They had to struggle to get the God from back home to be the God at our church (and of course the old friends were not at our church; they were back home too). Some were able to connect with a new church and make our church an extension of the faith that began back home, and some couldn't. The idea that God stays in one place is not as remote to us as we like to pretend.

Could God's Area of Influence Move or Expand?

During the eleven months that the Hebrews camped at the foot of Sinai, a tabernacle was erected. The creation of the tabernacle was an essential piece in our lesson. In the minds of the people, God lived on top of Sinai. Now an idea was being put into place.

No longer did God dwell atop Sinai in the smoke and clouds. Now God dwelled in the tabernacle. G. Henton Davies has a summary statement about the ark that helped me: "It was the place at which the God of Israel revealed himself to and dwelt among his people. It also housed the ark and accompanied Israel during the wilderness period. It is stated that it was located in several places in Canaan after Israel's settlement in that land and finally was replaced by Solomon's temple. It was this Israel's portable sanctuary from Sinai to Solomon's temple" (*The Interpreter's Dictionary of the Bible*, R–Z [New York: Abingdon Press, 1962], 498).

The tabernacle was a tent. Sometimes the tabernacle is called the "tent of meeting." It was the place where Yahweh met Moses, but note the change—God is no longer on top of a mountain. Now God has come nearer. God sits on the ark. God had moved from the top of the mountain to a tent at the base of the mountain.

Since the tabernacle was a tent, it could be moved. Our text reads, "the cloud lifted from over the tabernacle of the covenant" (10:11b). The cloud was a sign of God's presence. God was not only moving; God was leading. When Israel moved, she was actually *following* God. Moses met God at the "tent of meeting," got the instructions straight, and then "they set out for the first time at the command of the LORD by Moses" (10:13).

The insight that God could move does not bring us to New Testament understandings. Israel still saw Yahweh as their God; other tribes/nations had other gods. Monotheism would come later. But the new idea is "The Mobility of God." Inside this text are some ideas we may need to give a second look.

1. God was near. The "tent of meeting" was within sight of most of the people most of the time. They lived in the immediate presence of God. That idea will clean up your life.
2. Note the awe, the honor, the reverence in the text. With greatest care the route of procession is lined out. The tabernacle, ark, and "holy things" are handled like crown jewels. Special groups carried them. Those carriers were given priority in the arrangement of march. God's presence was never presumed or

treated as commonplace. It was the center of everything. The
ark was at the head of everything.

3. Hebrews didn't see themselves as being on a march, taking God
along with them. They saw God as active. When they began
their journey, Moses shouted, "Arise, O LORD, let your enemies
be scattered, and your foes flee before you" (10:35). God
charted the route. God went with them. God fought for them.
That kind of idea can put iron in the blood.

The God Who Is Singular and Ever-present

At this point I take liberty with the assignment. I'm going beyond
the text. If I stay tight to text, I will end this session deep in the
theological assumptions of a people who were only slowly
coming to understand God. The insights of the prophets would
enlarge and correct these assumptions, and that process would
go on for more than 1,000 years, until Jesus. Actually this session
is a study in the changing understandings of a people about God.
Our text is about the first time these people understood that
Yahweh could move.

We don't marvel that God can move. If we think, we know it.
But sometimes we do lock God into a sacred place, a place where
we have had good experiences with God. I want to fast-forward to
a New Testament text that sheds light on the question, "Where
does God live?"

Jesus was en route from Judea to Galilee; the short way was to
go through Samaria. They came to the Samaritan town of
Sychar; it was about noon. Jesus sat down by Jacob's well. A
Samaritan woman came to draw water; Jesus asked her for a
drink. She was surprised that he would open a conversation with
a Samaritan. The conversation began with a request for water
and moved to who Jesus was and "living water" (Jn 4:13-15). Jesus
suggested the woman call her husband. This was a delicate
subject; the woman had had five husbands, and the man she was
living with was not her husband. The woman tried to turn the
conversation by saying, "Sir I see that you are a prophet. Our
ancestors worshiped on this mountain, but you say that the place
where people must worship is in Jerusalem" (Jn 4:19-20). Where
does God dwell? Where is the right place to worship? Are the

Samaritans right? Does God live atop Mt. Gerizim? Or does God dwell in Jerusalem at the temple?

Jesus would have none of the old argument between Samaritans and Jews. He moved beyond "Where is God?" to another more profound idea: "The hour is coming, and is now here, when the true worshipers will worship the Father in spirit and truth, for the Father seeks such as these to worship him. God is spirit, and those who worship him must worship in spirit and truth" (Jn 4:23-24). Notice how far this is from Numbers:

- Moses led people to see that God could move from Sinai to the promised land.
- Now both Samaritan and Jesus know there is but one God; all other gods are false.
- God is not locked in a place; God is always near, omnipresent. There is no place God cannot reach. A temple or a sacred mountain may aid worship; neither is essential to worship. The important thing in making contact with God is not place, but the state of the heart. "In spirit and in truth" describes the earnest, honest appeal of a contrite soul. We don't find God; it is hard to get beyond the range of God's love.

It was Jesus who reassured his followers with these words: "Where two or three are gathered in my name, I am there among them" (Mt 18:19-20). And the parting line in Matthew's Great Commission is this: "And remember, I am with you always, to the end of the age" (Mt 28:20b). So where is God? The God we know in Christ is near. It does not matter where we are, what time of day it is, in whose company we find ourselves. . . God is near. God is more than mobile; if I meet the "in spirit and in truth" test, God is as near as a prayer.

Conclusion

Though it was many years ago, I remember well the surprise I felt when I got my first pair of glasses. I was in the fourth grade and assumed I saw what everyone else saw. I remember putting on those glasses, though, and being amazed at how clearly I could see. There were actually leaves on the trees and smiles on the faces! I had missed many of life's details without knowing it.

Wouldn't it be helpful (though painful!) if we could do the same thing with the sin in our lives? We could put on spiritual glasses and exclaim, "I never saw that as lust before!" Or "I never knew that was gluttony!" We would see our sin as sin, and we would be able to repent and be made whole.

Perhaps this study of the seven deadly sins can be those glasses for us. Perhaps it will help us see ourselves more clearly than we have in a long time.

Notes

Notes

2

THE REPUTATION OF GOD

Numbers 14:1-23

Central Question

How does God's reputation further the cause of missions?

Scripture

Numbers 14:1-23 Then all the congregation raised a loud cry, and the people wept that night. 2 And all the Israelites complained against Moses and Aaron; the whole congregation said to them, "Would that we had died in the land of Egypt! Or would that we had died in this wilderness! 3 Why is the LORD bringing us into this land to fall by the sword? Our wives and our little ones will become booty; would it not be better for us to go back to Egypt?" 4 So they said to one another, "Let us choose a captain, and go back to Egypt." 5 Then Moses and Aaron fell on their faces before all the assembly of the congregation of the Israelites. 6 And Joshua son of Nun and Caleb son of Jephunneh, who were among those who had spied out the land, tore their clothes 7 and said to all the congregation of the Israelites, "The land that we went through as spies is an exceedingly good land. 8 If the LORD is pleased with us, he will bring us into this land and give it to us, a land that flows with milk and honey. 9 Only, do not rebel against the LORD; and do not fear the people of the land, for they are no more than bread for us; their protection is removed from them, and the LORD is with us; do not fear them." 10 But the whole congregation threatened to stone them. Then the glory of the LORD appeared at the tent of meeting to all the Israelites. 11 And the LORD said to Moses, "How long will this people despise me? And how long will they refuse to believe in me, in spite of all the signs that I have done among them?

12 I will strike them with pestilence and disinherit them, and I will make of you a nation greater and mightier than they." 13 But Moses said to the LORD, "Then the Egyptians will hear of it, for in your might you brought up this people from among them, 14 and they will tell the inhabitants of this land. They have heard that you, O LORD, are in the midst of this people; for you, O LORD, are seen face to face, and your cloud stands over them and you go in front of them, in a pillar of cloud by day and in a pillar of fire by night. 15 Now if you kill this people all at one time, then the nations who have heard about you will say, 16 'It is because the LORD was not able to bring this people into the land he swore to give them that he has slaughtered them in the wilderness.' 17 And now, therefore, let the power of the LORD be great in the way that you promised when you spoke, saying, 18 'The LORD is slow to anger, and abounding in steadfast love, forgiving iniquity and transgression, but by no means clearing the guilty, visiting the iniquity of the parents upon the children to the third and the fourth generation.' 19 Forgive the iniquity of this people according to the greatness of your steadfast love, just as you have pardoned this people, from Egypt even until now." 20 Then the LORD said, "I do forgive, just as you have asked; 21 nevertheless —as I live, and as all the earth shall be filled with the glory of the LORD— 22 none of the people who have seen my glory and the signs that I did in Egypt and in the wilderness, and yet have tested me these ten times and have not obeyed my voice, 23 shall see the land that I swore to give to their ancestors; none of those who despised me shall see it."

Reflecting

As the father of three teenage daughters, I spend many of my Saturdays at the local shopping mall. I am allowed to drive the girls to the mall. I am allowed to walk with them into the mall. But I am not allowed to walk with them once we enter the hallowed halls of commerce.

Curious about this social phenomenon, I asked why I was not allowed to accompany them from store to store as I had in prior stages of life. Their response? It was because of the way I dressed.

I was accused of having evolved into a fashion disaster. They were embarrassed of ensembles that included wrinkled T-shirts and khakis or dress shoes with blue jeans or striped shirts with checked Bermuda shorts (particularly when accompanied by dress socks and tennis shoes).

I tried to explain the fact that I am forty-one years old, married, comfortable, and could care less what other people think of my attire. My oldest daughter, presumably speaking for the whole fashion-conscious family tree, simply stated, "We have reputations to protect."

It's easy to imagine teenagers being concerned with their reputations. It's harder to imagine the sovereign God considering personal reputation. However, the protection of God's divine reputation might be what allows missions efforts to continue in our world.

Remembering

In our last session, the children of Israel prepared for and began their journey away from Mt. Sinai toward the promised land. Their stay at Mt. Sinai had lasted approximately eleven months and covered the scope of biblical text from Exodus 19 to Numbers 10. During those months and chapters, the Israelites constructed the ark, tabernacle, altar, and priestly vestments. They also received the Law of God through Moses.

In Numbers 10:12, the Israelites set out to find and claim the land God promised to their ancestors. They were anxious to inhabit the land that had inhabited their dreams during the many years of Pharaoh's rule. God is faithful to the divine promise. In the Numbers narrative, Israel moves from Sinai to the promised land (Canaan) quickly.

Then, God instructed Moses to send scouts into the land (Num 13:1). We can almost taste the milk and smell the honey as the twelve Israelite spies leave the camp and head for Canaan. But what happens next becomes a pivotal point in Israel's history. The spies returned with an unfavorable majority report. Ten of the twelve spies warned, "We are not able to go up against this people" (Num 13:31). Only two, Joshua and Caleb, were willing to encourage God's people to occupy the land God promised.

In this moment when God's mission seems thwarted, we see an interesting facet of God's nature. God's commitment to being a God of power, grace, and mercy, enables the mission to continue through these people.

Studying

The Complaint of the People, 14:1-4 This was not the first time the Israelites complained, nor would it be the last. The cycle of complaint begins just verses after their departure from Egypt. In Exodus 13:17, Pharaoh releases the Israelite slaves. In 14:11, the complaints begin. They moan and groan in Exodus 16 and again in Exodus 17.

Rather than meet the challenges and demands inherent in God's mission for them to occupy the promised land, the Israelites expressed a desire to go back to Egypt. They asserted that death or slavery in Egypt would be more tolerable than the challenge set before them. They did not want to go up against unreasonable odds. They did not trust that God would fulfill the promise. In just a few sentences of cynicism, Israel rejected all that God had done (and would continue to do) for them. And this complaining was not from just one or two negative individuals. This was the sentiment of "all the congregation" (v. 1), "all the Israelites" (v. 2), and "the whole congregation" (v. 2).

> The idea of "returning to Egypt" serves as a strong symbol of apostasy and alienation from God in the Old Testament. This is evidenced in Hosea 7:11, Isaiah 30:1-7, Jeremiah 2:18, and Ezekiel 17:15. (Budd, 155).

The Encouragement of the Faithful, 14:5-10 Seeing the enormous consensus achieved by the negative report of most of the spies, Moses and Aaron assumed a posture of repentance before the people. There is no doubt Moses and Aaron sensed that divine wrath was about to explode upon them (Olson, 79). Caleb and Joshua were also aware of the dangers of unfaithfulness. These faithful few used practical and theological arguments to attempt

to encourage the people's commitment toward God and occupying the
land God promised.

Caleb and Joshua disagreed with
the assessment of the majority of the
spies. They reported that the land
should not be perceived as strong,
fortified, and devouring in nature, as
was conveyed in Numbers 13:28, 32.
Rather, they saw a land and a people who could be conquered.
Joshua and Caleb were extremely vivid in their opposing position
that "they are no more than bread for us" (14:9).

The spies said,
"They are stronger
than we" (Num
13:31). "Than we"
(mimenu) could also be
understood "than He." What
the spies suggested was that
even God could not overcome
the Canaanites.

More important, however, is their theological argument. The
faithful few believed that God was with them. Victory was not
dependent upon the power of humanity, but upon the presence
of God. The real question was not who is taller or who has more
weapons, but who trusts in the God of Israel? God's people were
questioning God's power, not their own. Refusing to enter the
land equaled rebellion.

These words of encouragement did not persuade the people to
take up weapons against the Canaanites. Rather, it incited them
to lift stones against Joshua and Caleb.

The Anger of God, 14:10-12 An agonizing and angry God met
Israel at the tent of meeting. God's agony is revealed in the questions raised in verse 11. God's use of the phrase "How long?"
places God's speech and emotions within the boundaries of
lament—speech that expresses the reality of disorientation, pain,
and loss. These "How long?" questions will remain all too familiar to the children of Israel. They are cried out during Egyptian
bondage, Assyrian siege, and
Babylonian exile. The prophets and
the psalmists will use these words to
express the deepest agonies felt by
humanity. At the tent of meeting,
God verbalized divine agony, lament-
ing, "How long?"

"A church that
goes on singing
'happy songs' in the
face of raw reality is
doing something very different
from what the Bible itself does"
(Brueggemann, 52). Even God
laments.

In the text, God's agony quickly
moves to anger. The climax of this

holy conversation is the twofold sentence of death and disinheritance. The pestilence that God intended to inflict upon Israel was a certain death sentence. God's pestilence will later be witnessed in 2 Samuel 24, Jeremiah 14, and Jeremiah 21. In each of theses cases, pestilence can simply be described as death (Budd, 158). Moses' words of appeal in verses 15 and 16 also support this concept. Moses thought God might "kill this people all at one time."

The death of the Israelites would naturally lead to their disinheritance of the promised land and promised favor of God. God, however, seemed determined to fulfill the promise through someone, so God chose Moses (v. 12b). Who could turn down such an offer? Moses could. Moses understood that the mission was more important than personal gain.

The Intercession of Moses, 14:13-19 Moses interceded for the people. His rationale for Israel's salvation was God's reputation. "What will the Egyptians say?" Moses asked. "What will the world think if the God of the Israelites destroys the Israelites?" Moses implied, in verse 14, that the news would spread like wildfire from Egypt to the inhabitants of Canaan, marring God's great reputation.

This divine reputation is anchored in two realities: God's power and God's merciful character. Moses argued that both were at stake in God's reaction to Israel's faithlessness. Destroying the Israelites would give the nations opportunity to suggest that God was not able to deliver the promised land to God's people. The nations could conclude that God was not strong enough to stand against the power of the Canaanites and their gods (Olson, 81). They could assume that the God who appeared as a cloud by day and a pillar of fire by night was something less than a warrior.

> "A man commits a crime—he should know better. We have him killed, and we feel pretty good about it. That's not power, though; that's justice. Justice is different than power. Power is when we have every justification to kill...and we don't."—Oskar Schindler to a Nazi officer in the film *Schindler's List*

On the flip side of power, Moses also appealed to the reputation of God's merciful character. The logic of Moses' argument is that God's reputation as a compassionate God would suffer if Israel perished (Levine, 366). God's "steadfast love" is mentioned some 250 times in the Old Testament (Riggans, 114). No other characteristic dominates the character of God like this one. In verse 19, Moses encourages God to be constant in character. God had always bent over backward, choosing love and forgiveness as primary reactions to God's people. Moses exhorted God to continue this pattern of mercy, practiced "from Egypt even until now." God's greatest strength—and the most unique characteristic of Israel's God—is the power to forgive.

The Continued Mission, 14:20-25 God maintained the consistency of God's character. Israel, as a nation, was forgiven, not because they deserved it, but because of who God is. A new nation would not be formed from the offspring of Moses. However, the individuals who refused to enter the promised land were sentenced to forty years in the wilderness. God's mercy, while dominant, cannot disregard necessary justice.

God's power was eventually conferred upon and enjoyed by a new generation. This new generation, symbolized by the faithfulness of Caleb and Joshua, inherited the promises of God. Through them, God's reputation of power and mercy remained intact.

Understanding

Israel continued to be a part of God's mission in the world because of God's character. God does care about people, but in God's agony and anger there arose the possibility of a people being annihilated and a new population arising from Moses. Israel's ultimate salvation was a result of God's reputation, not because they deserved God's favor.

Moses knew the power of arguing for God's reputation—it had worked in the past. God had threatened to abandon Israel and complete the divine mission through Moses once before. In Exodus 32, at the foot of Mt. Sinai, Israel constructed and worshiped a golden calf. God, seeing their transgression, threatened destruction and disinheritance. Moses, seeing God's anger, appealed to God's reputation.

Of course, God's reputation stretches farther than these two stories. It continues, throughout Scripture, to be a driving force for the mission of faith. When the Israelites finally entered the land of promise, Rahab the harlot had already heard of the powerful reputation of the God of Israel. The kings and rulers of Canaanite tribes had heard of the power of the God of Israel. Centuries later, when Israel demanded a king, God remained faithful to Israel (1 Sam 12:22). When the psalmist prayed for forgiveness, it was not for personal benefit, but for the sake of God's name (Ps 25:11; 79:9).

God even places the divine reputation on the line in the New Testament. When Jesus said, "When I am lifted up from the earth, [I] will draw all people to myself," he put the inherent power and mercy of God to the test. When Paul affirmed that "the gospel. . . is the power of God for salvation," the very reputation of God was at stake. The church's mission and her missions efforts have much to do with humanity, but they have much more to do with the glorification of God.

What About Me?

• *God has feelings, too.* It is too easy to presume that our actions have no impact on the heart of God. The opposite is true. Our selfishness, our complaints, and our faithlessness are an assault on the character and emotions of God.

• *We need to understand God's reputation.* It is often difficult to appeal to God's mercy on the basis of an individual's personal merits. We simply do not deserve mercy, but we need it. It is much easier to appeal to the character and promises of God.

• *Missions is about God.* The Israelites' refusal to enter the promised land was a missed opportunity for them to glorify God. They didn't trust God to fulfill the promise. Had they trusted God more, they could have witnessed the divine success of protection, provision, and fulfillment of purpose. In this instance, the world was not given a reason to praise and fear the God of

Israel. If we trusted God more, God's power could be more fully realized in our world. God continues to redeem the world through us, not because we deserve it, but because that's who God is.

Resources

Walter Brueggemann, *The Message of the Psalms* (Minneapolis: Augsburg Publishing House, 1984).

Philip J. Budd, *Numbers*, Word Biblical Commentary (Waco: Word, Incorporated, 1984).

Baruch A. Levine, "Numbers 1–20," *The Anchor Bible* (New York: Doubleday, 1993).

Dennis T. Olson, *Numbers*, Interpretation: A Bible Commentary for Teaching and Preaching (Louisville: John Knox Press, 1996).

Walter Riggans, *Numbers*, The Daily Study Bible Series (Louisville: Westminster John Knox Press, 1983).

THE REPUTATION OF GOD

Numbers 14:1-23

Introduction

"In the beginning. . . God created the heavens and the earth"
(Gen 1:1). Notice who started it all.

"Now the LORD said to Abram, 'Go from your country and
your kindred and your father's house to the land that I will show
you' " (Gen 12:1). God called Abraham.

Moses was keeping flocks in the desert, and from a burning
bush God said, "Moses, Moses!. . . I have observed the misery of
my people who are in Egypt. . . . And I have come down to deliver
them from the Egyptians, and to bring them up out of that land
to a good and broad land" (Ex 3:4, 7-8). God took them on as a
project.

The title for these sessions from Numbers is "Qualities of Our
Missional God." God is the source. I could press the idea of God's
taking the initiative a step further: "God so loved the world that
he gave his only Son, so that everyone who believes in him may
not perish but may have eternal life" (Jn 3:16). God has been
making the first move for a long time.

Today's session is a "test case." Can God take a people who
have strong opinions, who are guided more by their hunger and
fear than by any religious insight. . . can God get these people
from Egypt, through the wilderness, and into the promised land?
Can God finish what has been started? The subject in these sessions is the nature of God; Hebrew history is the setting for a
study in theology. Our title makes my point: "The Reputation of
God."

Numbers 13 is not our text, but it sets the stage. I hope you
will read about the twelve spies who were sent to check out the
promised land. They were sent at God's command (13:2) to see
what the land was like, check out the people who lived there,

determine if the towns were fortified, and bring back "some of the fruit of the land" (13:20b). Their report was mixed: "the land. . . flows with milk and honey. . . . Yet the people who live in the land are strong. . . . The land that we have gone through as spies is a land that devours its inhabitants; and all the people that we saw in it are of great size. . . . and to ourselves we seemed like grasshoppers" (13:27-33).

Report, Rebellion, and Leadership

The report of the twelve spies was not unanimous. Joshua and Caleb proposed immediate attack on Canaan with a view to possess it. Caleb said, "Let us go up at once and occupy it, for we are well able to overcome it" (13:30b). But that was not the majority opinion. The other ten said, "We are not able to go up against this people, for they are stronger than we" (13:31), and the majority opinion was the one taken by the people.

The effect of the report was devastating. "Then all the congregation raised a loud cry, and the people wept that night" (14:1). They had three complaints:

1. We need new leadership. "So they said to one another, 'Let us choose a captain, and go back to Egypt' " (14:4). They had lost confidence in their leadership; they were ready to replace them. This must have been a real threat, for Moses did not stand up, speak up, and brace them: "Then Moses and Aaron fell on their faces before all the assembly" (14:5a). The mission was at risk.
2. Better Egypt than our present mess. Life in the wilderness was desperately hard. It was blazing hot in the day; it was freezing cold at night. Manna kept them alive, but the diet was dull. Hostile tribes were all around them: "Why is the LORD bringing us into this land to fall by the sword? Our wives and our little ones will become booty; would it not be better for us to go back to Egypt?" (14:3). The price of freedom had become too high. Life was dearer than freedom to those people.
3. What is God doing? "Why is the LORD bringing us into this land to fall by the sword?" (14:3a) they asked. So soon they had forgotten that it was God who brought plagues to Egypt to break them free. The miracle at the Red Sea was out of their minds. Any prospect of being a free people was gone. They just

wanted out of the wilderness. Trusting God to fight their battles became "pie in the sky" talk.

Not everyone caved in to panic thinking. Joshua and Caleb stood firm and argued with the mob: "The land that we went through as spies is an exceedingly good land. If the LORD is pleased with us, he will bring us into this land and give it to us" (14:7b-8a). The sum of their argument was this:
• The land is good; it is worth the price we are paying to get it.
• We don't fight those people so much as God will fight for us. A better way to say it is, "God can win our battles for us." They tried to reason with a fearful, discouraged people, but Joshua and Caleb's words were ignored. The mob threatened to stone Moses and Aaron and head back to Egypt (14:10a). Things were out of hand.

God's First Response

"Then the glory of the LORD appeared at the tent of meeting to all the Israelites. And the LORD said to Moses, 'How long will this people despise me? And how long will they refuse to believe in me, in spite of all the signs that I have done among them? I will strike them with pestilence and disinherit them, and I will make of you a nation greater and mightier than they' " (14:10b-12).

Just when it seemed everything was going to fall apart. . . God's presence was made known!

1. "The glory of the LORD" is not meaningless, but it is mysterious. The footnotes in my annotated Bible gave this definition: "In the priestly view, 'the glory of the Lord' was an envelope of light (associated with the pillar of cloud and fire; see Ex 13:21-22) which veiled God's being. Though human beings could not see the Deity they could behold the glory that signified God's presence" (*The Oxford Annotated Bible* [New York: Oxford University Press, 1991], 90 OT section). It became clear to an unruly mob that they were in the immediate presence of God. This seemed to quiet them.
2. God was amazed at the ingratitude of the Israelites. They seemed to feel no sense of obligation.

3. God despaired of them and was ready to disinherit and destroy them. The complaints, the rebelliousness and fickleness, the inability to see the big picture. . . God had had enough.
4. God toyed with an idea. With the faithful few, God would raise up a new nation. I take it this would be the children of Moses and Aaron, of Joshua and Caleb. After Moses argued for mercy, God softened. But at the end of our text we will still see an edge in grace. Their near rebellion changed the destiny of thousands of people.

Moses Makes His Case

The three ideas that follow are the meat of the text. Two of those ideas are appeals Moses made to God. The last is God's response.
1. The Power Question: Can God get them to the promised land? "But Moses said to the LORD, 'Then the Egyptians will hear of it. . . and they will tell the inhabitants of this land. They have heard that you, O LORD, are in the midst of this people. . . . Now if you kill this people all at one time, then the nations who have heard about you will say, "It is because the LORD was not able to bring this people into the land he swore to give them that he has slaughtered them" ' " (14:13-16).

It is from this argument that we get the title for our session. "The reputation of God" was on the line in a world where arguments about whose god is the stronger were common. God had to work with people where they were. They lived in a world with many gods. The scene atop Mt. Carmel when Elijah had a "god contest" with the priests of Baal is a case in point (see 1 Kgs 18).

The sense of Moses' argument is this: If you don't get these people to the promised land, you are going to look weak to all who are watching. Moses reminded God that the pagan world was watching.
2. The Mercy Question: Will God forgive a rebellious people one more time? This appeal is one of the highest, noblest statements about the character of God found in the Old Testament. "And now, therefore, let the power of the LORD be great in the way that you promised when you spoke, saying, 'The LORD is slow to anger, and abounding in steadfast love, forgiving iniquity and transgression, but by no means clearing the guilty,

visiting the iniquity of the parents upon the children. . . . Forgive the iniquity of this people according to the greatness of your steadfast love, just as you have pardoned this people, from Egypt even until now' " (14:17-19).

The whole point of the Bible is to reveal God. At first people were afraid of God, but slowly there came into view a gentle, forgiving nature in Yahweh God. Moses lived 1,300 years before Jesus, but this text anticipated Jesus and the New Testament. In the later prophets, the idea of mercy and forgiveness appear often.

Moses pled with God. He appealed to God to display not wrath but mercy. He seems to say, "Can't you forgive them just one more time?" Moses did not make light of rebellion or play down the offense. He simply appealed to God to give them one more chance.

The church is often put in the place of God. Will we rise to kindness and mercy instead of judgment and severity? The answer seems obvious, but it is not an easy decision. If we always come down on "the side of the angels," we will finally tolerate serious sin in our company and stand for nothing. If we don't, we deny our noblest professions. God did not destroy and disinherit Israel from this incident. God forgave and continued the great mission of delivering them to the promised land. But the report of the spies and the rebellion that followed was "a fork in the road" for them.

3. The Justice Question: Now we hear God's response to Moses: "Then the LORD said, 'I do forgive, just as you have asked; nevertheless—as I live, and as all the earth shall be filled with the glory of the LORD—none of the people who have seen my glory and the signs that I did in Egypt and in the wilderness, and yet have tested me these ten times and have not obeyed my voice, shall see the land that I swore to give to their ancestors; none of those who despised me shall see it' " (14:20-23).

God's response to Moses' plea has three ideas:
• The mission will not be abandoned. God delivered the Israelites safely to the promised land. On this count, "the reputation of God" will be sustained by events. Egyptians, and any other

tribes who are watching, will see that God has the power to finish what God begins.

- God made a judgment on a generation. Israelites who came out of Egypt disappointed God one time too many: "None of the people who have seen my glory and the signs that I did in Egypt and in the wilderness, and yet have tested me these ten times and have not obeyed my voice, shall see the land that I swore to give to their ancestors" (14:22-23a). "Tested me these ten times" is not to be taken literally. It meant they had a pattern of "testing" God.

None of them would make it to the promised land: "all your number. . . from twenty years old and upward, who have complained against me, not one of you shall come into the land" (14:29-30). This is why the report of the spies was a turning point. God would wait for a new generation. Israel was consigned to the wilderness thirty-eight more years.

I have seen churches that have lived out this sentence. The old generation was so stuck in their ways that even the obvious evidence of the goodness of God could not convince them to move forward. They had to die off, and a new generation had to come forward, before anything could happen. This is not only history. It is script, and some churches are determined to live it. It takes a dab of faith to follow God in any generation, and if we don't show that spark, we lose our place in God's designs.

- God took note of the few who had faith. Exception was made for Joshua and Caleb and their families. They survived the years in the wilderness. They were given a large part in the victories that would come when Israel finally moved into the promised land.

There is both hope and warning in this text. God stayed on mission; God would not put up with faithlessness and rebellion indefinitely. If you think about it, a moral God acted morally. There is both grace and judgment in this session.

Notes

Notes

3

THE MERCY OF GOD

Numbers 21:1-9

Central Question

Is it possible for us to wander beyond the reach of God's grace?

Scripture

Numbers 21:1-9 When the Canaanite, the king of Arad, who lived in the Negeb, heard that Israel was coming by the way of Atharim, he fought against Israel and took some of them captive. 2 Then Israel made a vow to the LORD and said, "If you will indeed give this people into our hands, then we will utterly destroy their towns." 3 The LORD listened to the voice of Israel, and handed over the Canaanites; and they utterly destroyed them and their towns; so the place was called Hormah. 4 From Mount Hor they set out by the way to the Red Sea, to go around the land of Edom; but the people became impatient on the way. 5 The people spoke against God and against Moses, "Why have you brought us up out of Egypt to die in the wilderness? For there is no food and no water, and we detest this miserable food." 6 Then the LORD sent poisonous serpents among the people, and they bit the people, so that many Israelites died. 7 The people came to Moses and said, "We have sinned by speaking against the LORD and against you; pray to the LORD to take away the serpents from us." So Moses prayed for the people. 8 And the LORD said to Moses, "Make a poisonous serpent, and set it on a pole; and everyone who is bitten shall look at it and live." 9 So Moses made a serpent of bronze, and put it upon a pole; and whenever a serpent bit someone, that person would look at the serpent of bronze and live.

Reflecting

Okefenokee Joe is a living legend in the state of Georgia. Joe traipses through the woods, fields, and swamps of this broad state, enjoying the presence of snakes and learning about them. He leaves many of these mysterious reptiles in their habitat, undisturbed, and simply observes their behavior. Others he captures for use in his educational exhibitions and presentations.

Joe journeys to elementary schools, scout gatherings, television studios, and local festivals with his venomous valuables. He shares, in story and self-composed country songs, what he has learned about these legless wonders and their environments. While most of us flinch at the sight of these serpents, Joe respectfully handles the rattlers and moccasins and copperheads and rat snakes and king snakes in an effort to help us appreciate the role of these creatures within God's creation.

Okefenokee Joe has given his life to sharing the benefits of snakes with Southern society. But not even Okefenokee Joe could have imagined what a bronze snake would do for the wandering children of Israel.

Remembering

In last week's session, the children of Israel refused to enter Canaan—the land of promise. After receiving the law at Mt. Sinai and building necessary articles for worship, they saw God's promise fulfilled as they were led straight to the promised land. But a majority of the spies convinced a majority of the people that neither the military might of Israel nor the heavenly might of God would be able to conquer the land and its inhabitants.

This lack of faith led to a life sentence of wilderness wandering. The Israelites were divinely destined to meander through the wilderness until the whole generation died (Num 14–20). God's promise of land eventually was bestowed upon and enjoyed by a new generation of Israelites.

Numbers 14–20 is obviously an extremely negative portion of the exodus saga. Israel repeatedly rebelled against and resisted God's commands. God, in response, punished Israel with numerous plagues and military defeats. People died because of the plagues. People died because of battles. Miriam, Moses' sister, died. Aaron, Moses' brother and exodus comrade, died. One wonders if there is any hint of mercy left amid all this misery. Has Israel wandered beyond the possibility of hope? Is it possible for us to wander beyond the reach of God's grace?

Studying

Victory at Hormah, 14:1-3 The Israelites' successful military campaign in Numbers 21:1-3 comes as a surprise (Levine, 85). This episode of blessing is the first positive occurrence since Israel's refusal to enter the land of Canaan. The predominantly negative tone of wilderness wandering is interrupted for one significant moment.

This was not the first time Israel had found herself at Hormah. This particular place (whose name means "destruction") is first mentioned in Numbers 14:39-45—a text immediately following the story of the spies. When the Israelites realized the majority report of the spies was wrong and that God had sentenced them to wander in the wilderness, they decided to mount an attack on Canaan. Moses warned them that the Lord would not be with them. They attacked and were soundly defeated—at Hormah.

Now, in Numbers 21, the Israelites have wandered by the way of the Atharim. The king of Arad assaulted and captured some of the Israelites. Rather than go to war without God's blessing, the Israelites petitioned God concerning retaliation. Unlike their first war at Hormah, this time they followed the typical pattern for holy war: encounter with an enemy, a vow to dedicate all property to God through destruction, God's acceptance of the vow, God's handing over of the enemy, and Israel's fulfillment of the vow of destruction (Olson, 135).

> Many scholars believe the term *Atharim* may be understood as the Hebrew term *hatarim*, which means "the scouts." In this case, "the way of the Atharim" may refer to the path taken by the spies, in and out of Canaan, in Numbers 13:21-25. Israel had been down this road before...unsuccessfully (Plaut, 1160).

Israel's first visit to Hormah was a negative example of holy war. Israel's second journey down this path proved successful. It seems for the moment, at least for three verses, that Israel was starting to get it right. Maybe the march through the wilderness hadn't been pointless.

Mercy in the Wilderness, 14:4-9 Israel had battled in Hormah before. And believe it or not, Israel had complained before. Numbers 14:4-9 is one more complaint story in a long pattern of complaint stories associated with the exodus. It is, however, the last of the complaint narratives—and quite possibly the worst (Olson, 135).

Israel left Mt. Hor and journeyed around the land of Edom. As they traveled, the people again began to grumble. Their complaints were nothing new. In fact, the whole episode is hauntingly reminiscent of their first incident of complaint following their departure from Sinai. Both stories follow a pattern: complaint, divine punishment, confession, a request for Moses' intercession, and a prayer by Moses to dissuade God's threat (Dozeman, 163).

> Israel vowed to place the cities of Arad under a *herem* or ban. Under the ban, all enemy property would be considered devoted to God. All property would be given over to God through destruction rather than retained as spoils of war by the victorious warriors (Dozeman, 163).

The subjects of the complaints were not new. Israel seemed to carry a list of grievances to which they periodically referred. There was apparently no critical creativity in the camp. Verse 5 provides us with the same old issues: regret over the departure from Egypt, lack of water, and a monotonous menu. (The manna once considered a miraculous blessing was later viewed as a despised curse.) The only difference in this round of complaints is that, instead of only speaking against Moses as they had in prior texts, this time they spoke directly against God. Maybe that's why the punishment was so immediate and so severe.

In verse 6, the Lord sent poisonous or fiery serpents among the people. These agents of God bit and killed many of the people. It seems that God was soon to complete the wilderness purpose. After years of wandering, the last of the old generation was dying—one by one. Their journey had begun with faithless complaints, and they came full circle; their last complaints led to death. Or did they?

In verse 7, the people came to Moses (as was their predictable pattern) and asked him to intercede on their behalf. They acknowledged their sin and, in their pain, asked Moses to seek God's mercy on their behalf. They did not want to die.

Please allow me a few lines of writer's license. If I had been Moses, I would have told the Israelites, "I know you are dying. This is the moment for which we have been waiting and wandering. God sent you into the wilderness to die. We could have entered Canaan years ago, but you complained and we have wandered. Now it's time for you to die. So die!" Of course, I am not Moses.

Moses, as was his pattern, again prayed for the people. May I have a few more lines of writer's license? If I had been God, I would have screamed back at Moses, "I know they are dying. This is the moment for which you have been waiting and wandering. I sent them into the wilderness to die. Now they are dying. Let them die!" Of course, I am not God.

God's subsequent response to Moses' intercession goes beyond the boundaries of human nature. God's response goes against the intended wilderness purpose. God's response probably astonished the bitten Israelites—who fully expected to die. God responded with grace and mercy and life, which is God's pattern.

God instructed Moses to fashion a *seraph* (serpent figure) and to mount it on a pole. Moses constructed the figure from bronze. From that point on, when anyone was bitten by a serpent, if they looked at the bronze figure, they lived. They lived! Contrary to wilderness purpose, they lived.

Recognizing that this story occurs toward the end of the old generation's life and on the brink of a new generation's succession, who received the gift of life? One might conclude that only

> The Hebrew word *seraphim* is the basis for the translation "fiery serpent." *Seraph* (the singular form of *seraphim*) comes from the verb *saraph*, which means "to burn." There is no doubt that these creatures are divine agents of God and could possibly be equated with the temple creatures mentioned in Isaiah 6:2, 14:29, and 30:6 (Budd, 234).

In 2 Kings 18:4, King Hezekiah destroys a "bronze serpent that Moses had made" as part of his temple reform. Apparently, persons had begun making sacrifices to the serpent assuming it held some mystical power. The serpent story is also later remembered in Scripture by Jesus (Jn 3:14) and Paul (1 Cor 10:9) (Riggans, 159).

the new generation could receive the promise of life since the old generation had been sentenced to die. Within the Numbers narrative, however, the stories of the new generation do not begin until after the census in Numbers 26.

Some might suggest that this story, along with the victory at Hormah, serves as a lesson for the new generation. The old generation successfully engaged an enemy and survived a complaint in order to provide a new example of how the new generation should live (Olson, 134). This explanation, however, falls short of explaining how "life" can be promised to individuals in the old generation who are destined to die.

Could it be that God had again bent to grace and mercy? Could it be that salvation and life and entrance into the promised land were offered to the remnant who would look and believe? Was God giving the children of favor one last chance? Is God reminding us that we can never wander outside the reach of divine grace?

Understanding

Hope is an accurate description of God's nature as displayed in Numbers 21:1-9. For a generation destined to die, the possibilities of victory and life, which are afforded in these short verses, reopen the door to the future.

When Jesus talked with Nicodemus, in John 3, he used the story of the bronze serpent to portray the nature of his ministry. Speaking of his imminent crucifixion, Jesus drew a strong parallel between the ideas of belief and life. When Jesus was finally lifted up in death, he looked out upon Jews and Romans, rich and poor, men and women, and prayed, "Father, forgive them; for they do not know what they are doing" (Lk 23:34). Jesus interceded for a generation destined to die, just as Moses had before him. No one—*no one*—is beyond the reach of his prayer.

One of our greatest motivations for engagement in missions efforts is the mercy of God. There is no nation, no inner city, no rural town, no generation, no family, no cult, no people group, or no individual who has wandered so far into the wilderness that they are outside the reach of God's mercy and grace. If we lift up Christ, they will be drawn to victory, life, and the possibility of a new future.

What About Me?

• *Humanity is stuck in a sinful cycle.* The repetition of the Israelites' complaints and wars at Hormah are reflective of the shortcomings and battles we fight over and over again. We all need the mercy of God. What battles do we continually fight? What is

And just as Moses lifted up the serpent in the wilderness, so must the Son of Man be lifted up, that whoever believes in him may have eternal life. Jn 3:14-15

on our complaint list? How do we accept and offer the mercy of God?

- *The mercy of God prompts missions.* If there is no possibility of salvation from the wilderness cycles of life, then missions need not exist. But because God is merciful, and because no one is beyond God's merciful reach, the mission continues.

- *We are saved by the mercy of God.* Jesus did not come to judge or condemn the world. Jesus did not accuse from the cross. His life and his words were weighted with grace. Those who wandered under a death sentence in the wilderness desperately needed God's grace. Those of us who wander in the wilderness of this world need God's grace as well.

• *We serve by the mercy of God.* None of us deserves a place in the community of faith, the divine mission, or the promised land. We have simply looked, believed, and been accepted.

Resources

Philip J. Budd, *Numbers*, Word Biblical Commentary (Waco: Word, Incorporated, 1984).

Thomas B. Dozeman, "The Book of Numbers," *The New Interpreter's Bible* (Nashville: Abingdon Press, 1998).

Baruch A. Levine, *Numbers 1–20*, The Anchor Bible (New York: Doubleday, 1993).

Dennis T. Olson, *Numbers*, Interpretation: A Bible Commentary for Teaching and Preaching (Louisville: John Knox Press, 1996).

Gunther Plaut, *Numbers*, The Torah: A Modern Commentary (New York: The Union of American Hebrew Congregations, 1981).

Walter Riggans, *Numbers*, The Daily Study Bible Series (Louisville: Westminster John Knox Press, 1983).

THE MERCY OF GOD

Numbers 21:1-9

Introduction

Last week's session was from early wilderness adventures. Twelve spies were sent to explore the promised land. Their report changed the calendar, the players, and the setting. Wilderness time should have been a few months, maybe a year or two. Instead, it became home for Israel for forty years. God was not happy with their faithlessness: "According to the number of the days in which you spied out the land, forty days, for every day a year, you shall bear your iniquity, forty years, and you shall know my displeasure" (Num 14:34). And so they languished.

Today's text describes two incidents that happened in late wilderness. Because this material is so unfamiliar to me, I read chapters 10–21. It was discouraging reading. My comments will focus on our text, but I will use Numbers 10–21 as background. I occasionally came across the expression "stiff-necked." I thought it was an intemperate, unkind adjective. Reading Numbers changed my mind. God called the Hebrews "stiff-necked": "The LORD said to Moses, 'I have seen this people, how stiff-necked they are. Now let me alone, so that my wrath may burn hot against them' " (Ex 32:9-10a). The same idea appears in Exodus 33:5 and Deuteronomy 9:6, 13; 10:16. God aimed these references at the difficult generation Moses led out of Egypt. They were nearly impossible, and I have more sympathy for Moses from this reading. To get "a feel" for this material and the kind of people Moses was leading, I recommend these chapters. It changed the way I wrote this comment.

I will give slight attention to the first three verses of the text. They are introductory. The sum of those verses is this:
• Aaron has died atop Mount Hor (20:14-29). Moses is old and his time is short. The old generation is passing off the scene.

- Israel is on the move. They are getting in position to enter the promised land from the east.
- A Canaanite king named Arad learned the Israelites were approaching and blocked them as they advanced "by the way of Atharim." John J. Owens speculated, "From a knowledge of the terrain one would think that Atharim was the name of a mountain pass" (*The Broadman Bible Commentary*, vol. 2 [Nashville: Broadman Press, 1970], 137). A few Israelites were taken prisoner.
- Instead of rushing ahead of God as they had done before, this time the Israelites got it right. They made a vow to God: "If you will indeed give this people into our hands, then we will utterly destroy their towns" (21:2b).
- God "handed over the Canaanites," and Israel kept her promise: "they utterly destroyed them and their towns" (21:3b). This was the first success these people had had in a long time. They neither balked at God's leading nor rushed ahead of God; they moved in concert with God.

Now we come to the text I think is most applicable to us (21:4-9). You will notice the influence of incidents in Numbers 10–21. There is a pattern in this material, and that is a good place to start.

Tiresome Cycle

"From Mount Hor they set out by the way to the Red Sea, to around the land of Edom; but the people became impatient on the way. The people spoke against God and against Moses, 'Why have you brought us up out of Egypt to die in the wilderness? For there is no food and no water, and we detest this miserable food'" (21:4-5).

I took pencil in hand and counted the times Moses had trouble with the Hebrews in Numbers. Here is what I found.

- "Now when the people complained in the hearing of the LORD about their misfortunes, the LORD heard it" (Num 11:1).
- "While they were at Hazeroth, Miriam and Aaron spoke against Moses because of the Cushite woman whom he had married and they said, 'Has the LORD spoken only through Moses?

Has he not spoken through us also?' And the LORD heard it" (Num 12:1-2).

- The twelve spies returned; ten of the twelve said they must not attempt to enter Canaan: "Then all the congregation raised a loud cry, and the people wept that night. And all the Israelites complained against Moses and Aaron" (Num 14:1-2a).
- Korah, Dathan, and Abiram took 250 "Israelite men, and they confronted Moses. They assembled against Moses and against Aaron, and said to them, 'You have gone too far!' " (Num 16:1-3).
- "Now there was no water for the congregation; so they gathered together against Moses and against Aaron. The people quarreled with Moses" (Num 20:2-3a).
- And then we come to our text: "From Mount Hor they set out by the way to the Red Sea, to go around the land of Edom; but the people became impatient on the way. The people spoke against God and against Moses" (Num 21:4-5a).

I've piled illustration upon illustration to make a point. Those people were difficult. Their complaints were these:
1. God has let us down. God is not making good on the promise to get us to the promised land.
2. Moses is high-handed. This idea surfaced several times.
3. We'd be better off in Egypt.
4. Water is scarce, and the food is monotonous.

Complaining is a habit. It is negative and faith-consuming. When a people get into the complaining cycle, it is hard to coax them out of it. In the last ten years I've visited many churches. A few of them have a pattern of complaining. In fact, I visited a church that had fallen out with every preacher they had had since 1950. The property was in disrepair. The membership was shriveled. The fellowship was nonexistent. The reputation of the church was known; intelligent people drove to the next church. Who wants to join a negative, complaining people who are wallowing in their distemper?

Our text does not give a remedy for this disease of the spirit. It simply chronicles the people's outbursts as a kind of signpost for us. The text shouts at us: *this is not the way to be*! If your church is the complaining kind, use this text to bring about change.

Endless Mercy

"Then the LORD sent poisonous serpents among the people, and they bit the people, so that many Israelites died. The people came to Moses and said, 'We have sinned by speaking against the LORD and against you; pray to the LORD to take away the serpents from us.' So Moses prayed for the people. And the LORD said to Moses, 'Make a poisonous serpent, and set it on a pole; and everyone who is bitten shall look at it and live.' So Moses made a serpent of bronze, and put it upon a pole; and whenever a serpent bit someone, that person would look at the serpent of bronze and live" (21:6-9).

The picture we get of God in Numbers is muddled.

1. The complaints of the people usually angered God. When the people complained in 11:1, "the LORD heard it and his anger was kindled. Then the fire of the LORD burned against them, and consumed some outlying parts of the camp" (11:1b). In our text, "the LORD sent poisonous serpents among the people, and they bit the people, so that many Israelites died" (21:6). God's judgment could be severe. It is true to say that one facet of the character of God is mercy, but there is judgment in this story too.

2. Sometimes it appears Moses softened and tempered the wrath of God. The first response was wrath; the considered response was mercy. I don't know what to do with this pattern except to reason that those people didn't have nearly as much Bible (and experience with God) as we do. They didn't have Jesus.

3. Finally, the mercy of God makes forgiveness seem too easy. The cycle of (1) sin, (2) wrath, (3) Moses' intercession, and (4) God's relenting is repeated several times. This story is like the prodigal son story in Luke 15. Repentance and grace are made automatic and without price. In this text a bronze serpent was made, put on a tall pole, and all who were bitten by poisonous serpents could look "at the serpent of bronze and live" (21:9). It was as easy as that. Sounds like an evangelist. All you have to do to be a Christian is just "believe in Jesus." And if you try to

add qualifiers or conditions, you "don't believe the Bible." If you use all of the Bible, you will notice that two conditions are always attached to God's mercy:

• Obedience was expected; without it, mercy would be withdrawn.
• An exalted ethic was expected of the people who were God's chosen. An ethical God expected ethical conduct.

Again and again God overlooked, pardoned, and forgave a complaining, faithless people. Again and again God took them back when they misbehaved. The people who complained, who kept backing away from obedience and faith—those people did not get to the promised land. And to put an exclamation point on this, note that even Moses did not make it. God did show mercy, but that was not the whole story.

Anticipating Jesus

"So Moses made a serpent of bronze, and put it upon a pole; and whenever a serpent bit someone, that person would look at the serpent of bronze and live" (21:9).

"And just as Moses lifted up the serpent in the wilderness, so must the Son of Man be lifted up, that whoever believes in him may have eternal life. For God so loved the world that he gave his only Son, so that everyone who believes in him may not perish, but may have eternal life" (Jn 3:14-16). Jesus was talking to Nicodemus. He was trying to explain to Nicodemus who he was and what he came to do. He reached back into Numbers and used our text to communicate. What does this mean to us? At this point I offer an interpretation.

1. Our condition is like the Israelites in the wilderness. We are confused. Often we complain. We can't see the larger design of God, and we are impatient with God's calendar. Our ways invite judgment. Our sins have wounded us, and, if left unattended, will kill us. We are snake-bitten.

2. Moses reached back into Egyptian lore: "Since the Israelites had lived so long in Egypt, they had observed the Egyptian use of the serpent symbol as a repellent for the biting serpents" (John J. Owens, *The Broadman Bible Commentary*, vol. 2, 139). The bronze serpent was lifted high. Healing came when the

people looked. Was this sympathetic magic or faith? The text is clear: "And the LORD said to Moses, 'Make a poisonous serpent, and set it on a pole; and everyone who is bitten shall look at it and live' " (21:8). God suggested the symbol, and God did the healing. Hundreds of years later another symbol was raised high on a Roman cross. The bronze serpent was a temporary solution for a temporary crisis. Jesus is a permanent answer to a universal problem. Again, it was God who permitted the cross, and it is God's way to heal a broken humankind.

3. "Look and live" is literal. What is underneath this symbol? The answer is faith. We, like so many Israelites, are hurting. Jesus is high and lifted up on Calvary's cross. When we look in faith, God makes us whole.

4. It is the mission of the church to "lift up Jesus," to call attention to Jesus, to witness the words and works of Jesus, to live and die in imitation of Jesus. Like Paul in Corinth, we need to concentrate our gospel: "For I decided to know nothing among you except Jesus Christ, and him crucified" (1 Cor 2:2).

At this point I've gone beyond the text, but all the great interpreters see Numbers 21:9 as a signpost pointing to another and greater who also was lifted up. All of the Old Testament was in anticipation of Jesus. This text points to the witness of Jesus and the church; it is a preview of grace and salvation for all humankind. It is about "the mercy of God."

Notes

Notes

4

THE PROMISES OF GOD

Numbers 34

Central Question

How do the promises of God keep missions alive?

Scripture

Numbers 34 The LORD spoke to Moses, saying: 2 Command the Israelites, and say to them: When you enter the land of Canaan (this is the land that shall fall to you for an inheritance, the land of Canaan, defined by its boundaries), 3 your south sector shall extend from the wilderness of Zin along the side of Edom. Your southern boundary shall begin from the end of the Dead Sea on the east; 4 your boundary shall turn south of the ascent of Akrabbim, and cross to Zin, and its outer limit shall be south of Kadesh-barnea; then it shall go on to Hazar-addar, and cross to Azmon; 5 the boundary shall turn from Azmon to the Wadi of Egypt, and its termination shall be at the Sea. 6 For the western boundary, you shall have the Great Sea and its coast; this shall be your western boundary. 7 This shall be your northern boundary: from the Great Sea you shall mark out your line to Mount Hor; 8 from Mount Hor you shall mark it out to Lebo-hamath, and the outer limit of the boundary shall be at Zedad; 9 then the boundary shall extend to Ziphron, and its end shall be at Hazar-enan; this shall be your northern boundary. 10 You shall mark out your eastern boundary from Hazar-enan to Shepham; 11 and the boundary shall continue down from Shepham to Riblah on the east side of Ain; and the boundary shall go down, and reach the eastern slope of the sea of Chinnereth; 12 and the boundary shall go down to the Jordan, and its end shall be at the Dead Sea. This shall be your land with its boundaries all around. 13 Moses commanded the Israelites, saying: This is the land that you shall inherit by lot, which the LORD has commanded to give to the nine tribes and to the half-tribe; 14 for the tribe of the Reubenites by their ancestral houses and the tribe of the Gadites by their ancestral houses have taken their inheritance, and also the half-tribe of Manasseh; 15 the two tribes and the half-tribe have taken their inheritance beyond the Jordan at Jericho eastward, toward the sunrise. 16 The LORD spoke to Moses, saying: 17 These are the names of the men who shall apportion the land to you for inheritance: the priest Eleazar and Joshua son of Nun. 18 You shall take one leader of every tribe to apportion the land for inheritance. 19 These are the names of the men: Of the tribe of Judah, Caleb son of Jephunneh. 20 Of the tribe of the Simeonites, Shemuel son of Ammihud. 21 Of the tribe of Benjamin, Elidad son of Chislon. 22 Of the tribe of the Danites a leader, Bukki son of Jogli. 23 Of the Josephites: of the tribe of the Manassites a leader, Hanniel son of Ephod, 24 and of the tribe of the Ephraimites a leader, Kemuel son of Shiphtan. 25 Of the tribe of the Zebulunites a leader, Elizaphan son of Parnach. 26 Of the tribe of the Issacharites a leader, Paltiel son of Azzan. 27 And of the tribe of the Asherites a leader, Ahihud son of Shelomi. 28 Of the tribe of the Naphtalites a leader, Pedahel son of Ammihud. 29 These were the ones whom the LORD commanded to apportion the inheritance for the Israelites in the land of Canaan.

Reflecting

I have read through the Bible twice. Once, I was in my twenties and decided to reacquaint myself with the whole of Christian Scripture. I was amazed by the many stories I had missed or forgotten through the years. I was further amazed by the details I had ignored in many more familiar stories. It was a lengthy but enriching experience to explore the cracks and crevices of my faith canon.

My first adventure through the entire text, however, was during my elementary school years. My parents made a commitment at church to read the Bible in one year. Each night, our family of six would gather in the den for the daily apportioned chapters. We were typically captivated by the stories of Adam and Eve and Noah and Abraham and Samuel and David and Solomon. On the other hand, some texts left us nearly catatonic. Levitical laws, genealogies, and land disbursements were not intended to be read to children after 9:00 p.m. I guess my first thorough reading of the Bible doesn't count. . . since I slept through parts of it.

Numbers 34 contains a delineation of the boundaries of the land of Canaan, as well as the designated leaders of the Israelite tribes that would inhabit the region. If you choose to read this text in the late evening, you may find it beneficial with regard to your chronic insomnia. Read it when you are a bit more alert, and it may add to your understanding of missions.

Remembering

Numbers 26 describes a census taken of a new generation. The wilderness wandering had come to an end. The complainers, the faithless warriors, and those who refused to "look and live" died.

Not only did individuals die, but memories died with them. The vast majority, the faithless majority, took the memories of Egypt to their graves. There were few left who could say, "It was better for us in Egypt"—and those who could say it wouldn't.

This new generation had only heard stories of Egypt. They celebrated Passover, Pentecost, and Booths in order to keep the story alive. But this generation was born in the wilderness. The wilderness was all they knew. Manna, quail, and water were their physical sustenance. Their emotional sustenance had been a dream of a land of promise. All their lives they longed to taste milk and honey. Their imaginations ran wild on those occasions

The three pilgrimage feasts of Passover, Pentecost, and Booths successively tell the story of the exodus. Passover commemorates the escape from Egypt; Pentecost commemorates the giving of the Law at Sinai; and Booths commemorates the wilderness experience. These holy days convey the significant moments of Israel's history in the same way Christmas, Epiphany, Good Friday, and Easter recount the pivotal events of Christian faith.

when Joshua and Caleb told them of pomegranates, figs, and clusters of grapes so large they had to be carried on a pole between two men.

The mission was kept alive through God's promises. God's people heard, imagined, and recited what lay ahead. These promises were worth believing. They were promises worth working toward. They were promises that provided hope to wilderness children.

Studying

Real Boundaries, 34:1-15 The first fifteen verses of Numbers 34 convey to the new generation of Israelites the boundaries of Canaan. At the command of God, Moses communicated these boundaries to the Israelites. It is clear that the land was given, measured, and eventually settled according to the plan of God. But how was Moses able to define clearly territorial boundaries and landmarks without ever having been through the region? Of course, God could have provided this detailed demarcation of Canaan. Two surviving spies, Joshua and Caleb, however, may have aided God's general instruction.

Verses 3-12 record the names of specific sites necessary for determining the boundaries of the promised land. The Wilderness of Zin served as the southern boundary. The Great Sea (Mediterranean) served as the western boundary. The northern region reached as far a Lebo-hamath (about 100 miles north of Tyre and Sidon), and the Jordan River served as the eastern boundary. This particular delineation of borders closely follows the description of the area examined by the spies in Numbers 13–14. These borders suggest that Joshua and Caleb may have been of some assistance in determining the boundaries of the land. This duplication of boundaries also communicated assurance to the new generation that the original land of promise had truly been extended to them in its entirety (Olson, 187).

The expanse of these boundaries far exceeds the area of land that Israel controlled through most of her later history. These boundaries represent, to a great extent, an idealized territory that Israel never entirely occupied (Budd, 367). Often our promised

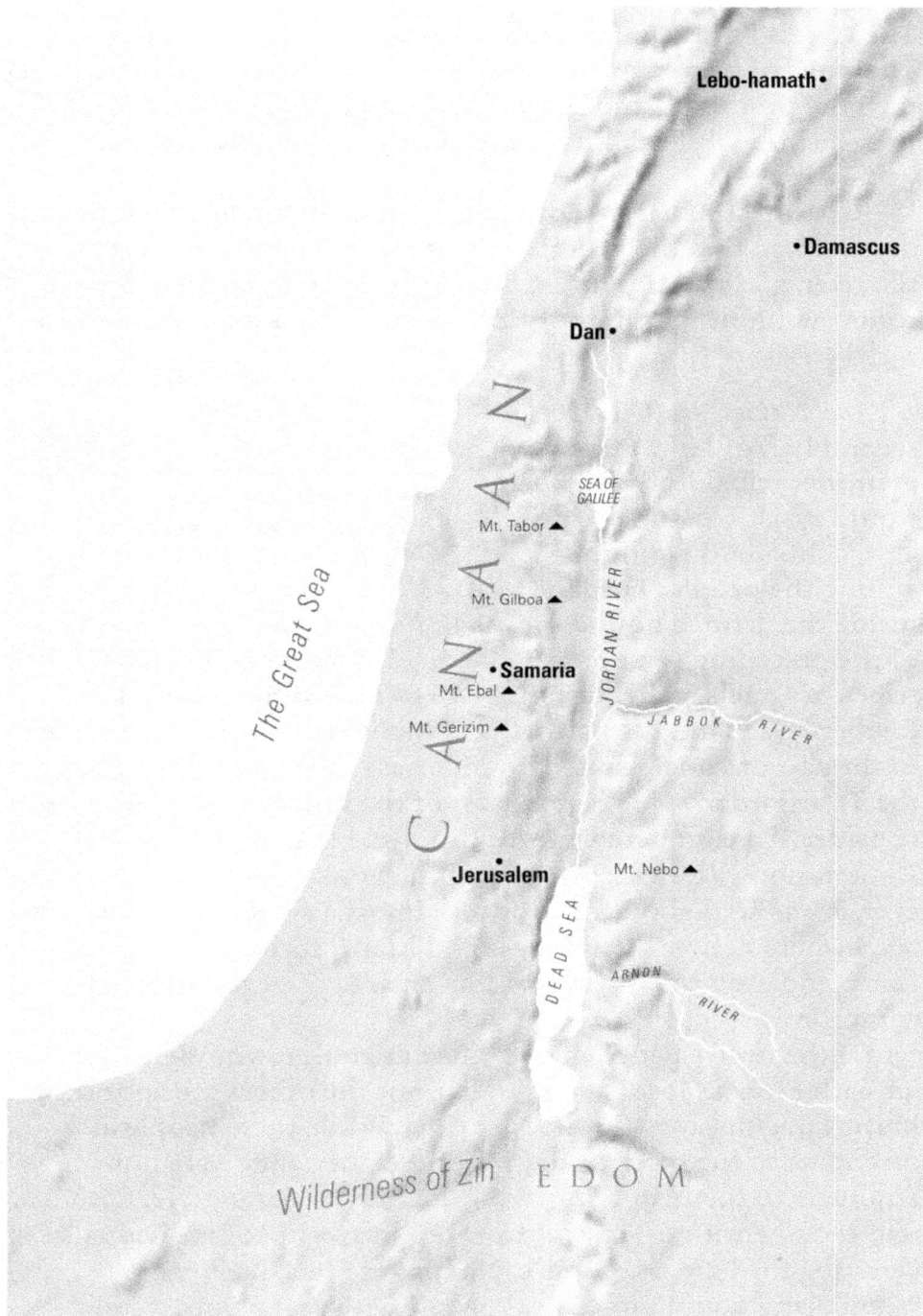

Lebo-hamath •

• Damascus

Dan •

C A N A A N

SEA OF
GALILEE

Mt. Tabor ▲

Mt. Gilboa ▲

JORDAN RIVER

• **Samaria**
Mt. Ebal ▲

Mt. Gerizim ▲

JABBOK   RIVER

•**Jerusalem**   Mt. Nebo ▲

DEAD SEA

ARNON
RIVER

The Great Sea

Wilderness of Zin   E D O M

lands are colored and filled by all we lack in our present land. The streets of heaven are gold. The gates of heaven are pearl. The walls of heaven are jasper. The new generation of Israel imagined the promised land to be everything the wilderness wasn't. It was the idea and ideal that kept them going for years in the wilderness.

Regardless of the breadth of their imagining, however, we must affirm that the promised land was real. The sites, the sea, the river, and the mountains were real. This new land was not some nebulous idea in the mind of God. It was a carefully delineated territory (Budd, 369).

Real Names, 34:16-29 The second half of Numbers 34 identifies tribal leaders who would assist Eleazar, the priest, and Joshua in dividing the land among the people. The land inside the defined boundaries of the preceding verses was to be divided among nine-and-a-half tribes of Israel. Earlier, verses 14-15 indicated the tribes of Reuben, Gad, and the half-tribe of Manasseh would receive land to the east of Israel's stated boundaries—an area referred to as the Transjordan. This region, east of the Jordan River, was considered a conquered part of promised land in the book of Deuteronomy (Deut 2:24). Within the book of Numbers, however, it was settled yet fluid. It was almost a symbolic region—somewhere between wilderness and home. Its borders were a bit fuzzy, and even today it represents an area of negotiation and compromise (Olson, 188).

While the tribe of Levi was not apportioned tribal land within the boundaries of Canaan (see Num 35:1-8; Josh 13:14; 21), there were still twelve tribal regions. This was a result of land being dispensed to Manasseh and Ephraim, the two sons of Joseph.

Of the twelve people listed, most are unknown. We are familiar with Eleazar, Joshua, and Caleb, but the others are appearing in the Israelite story for the first time. While these people are unknown to the modern-day biblical reader, they were not strangers to their community. These men were tangible, flesh-and-blood entities. They represented the reality of individuals claiming the land of promise. No longer was Israel just a "wandering population." Real people with real names were preparing to enter Canaan.

The designation of these leaders also reflects a sense of future purpose in the life of Israel. They were given a job within the boundaries of the land of promise. Prior to Numbers 34, the Israelites' purpose was little more than survival. Wilderness tasks defined their existence. They gathered manna. They searched for water. They struggled to secure campsites. They moved their provisions. But now, leaders were appointed in anticipation of future realities. While food, water, shelter, and protection were still valid concerns, Israelite life was no longer absorbed by daily tasks alone. The people productively and proactively worked toward a dream.

There are three lists of twelve leaders in the book of Numbers. The first is in Numbers 1—twelve supervisors enlisted to carry out the first census. The second list is in Numbers 13—twelve spies chosen to scout the promised land. This final list, in Numbers 34, names those who provided leadership for the occupation and settling of Canaan. Each list of names came at pivotal points in the wilderness story (Olson, 188). This final list, however, represents the most celebrative moment—real people who would lead Israel toward the realization of their dream.

Understanding

In his classic work *The Prophetic Imagination*, Walter Brueggemann stated, "The task of prophetic ministry is to nurture, nourish, and evoke a consciousness and perception alternative to the consciousness and perception of the dominant culture around us" (13). This may well be the heart, soul, and goal of all missions work. The community of faith and individuals within the faith are called to present an alternative reality to our world.

Moses presented such a reality to the enslaved Israelites. While they labored under Egyptian oppression, he inspired their imaginations with alternative realities: "The Lord will pass through to strike down the Egyptians" (Ex 12:23) and "The Egyptians whom you see today, you shall never see again" (Ex 14:13) and "The Lord will reign forever and ever" (Ex 15:13). These and many other messages evoked the dream of a world where the power of Pharaoh is vanquished and the power of God is revealed.

In Numbers 34, Moses again inspired the imagination of the Israelites. With an indistinguishable blending of the fabled promised land and the concrete list of sites and names, he helped the community of faith envision an alternative reality to their present wilderness.

As Brueggemann suggested, the prophets also did this. Years later, when Israel was exiled in Babylon, the promises of God enabled them to envision better days to come: "Everyone who thirsts, come to the waters; and you that have no money, come, buy and eat! Come, buy wine and milk without money and without price" (Isa 55:1). God's promises become the source of dreams and messages and missions action.

Jesus prompts our imaginations in the same fashion. He set before us the promises of a kingdom—a kingdom that is simultaneously before us and with us, a kingdom defined by love in the present and eternal life in the future. The boundaries of this promised kingdom are real. The inhabitants' names are those of our ancestors, our saints, our family, our friends, ourselves, and anyone else who embraces the dream. It is a promised reality to all who move through the wilderness. . . and believe.

What About Me?

• *Missions efforts help the world imagine a new reality.* When we engage the world with the gospel message and gospel action, we embody and proclaim a different world—a counterculture— a new way to live. The world is given a glimpse of the way things could be. . . and will be.

• *At times, only the promise of an alternative reality keeps us moving in the wilderness.* The dream of promised land not only gives hope to the world, but is a source of strength for the community of faith.

• *The kingdom of heaven is more than just a dream.* The boundaries of promised land are real. The inhabitants of promised land are real. The kingdom of God, in this life and the next, is tangible and accessible.

• *The promises of God provide purpose within and beyond the daily tasks of life.* The missions life is not monotonous. Every moment and every task becomes an opportunity to imagine and live life differently. We are working toward a new reality.

Resources

Walter Brueggemann, *The Prophetic Imagination* (Philadelphia: Fortress Press, 1978).

Philip J. Budd, *Numbers*, Word Biblical Commentary (Waco: Word, Incorporated, 1984).

Baruch A. Levine, *Numbers 1–20*, The Anchor Bible (New York: Doubleday, 1993).

Dennis T. Olson, *Numbers*, Interpretation: A Bible Commentary for Teaching and Preaching (Louisville: John Knox Press, 1996).

THE PROMISES OF GOD

Numbers 34

Introduction

Numbers 34 is not easy reading. The text seems so remote to us. It helps us understand an emerging nation, but there is little food for the soul. Anyone who writes on this text is going to have to use some imagination.

I began reading at Numbers 21:1, the starting place for last week's session, and read through chapter 34. From Numbers 10–21, there is a negative, complaining, rebellious, troublesome people. Chapter 21 is a turn in the road for those people. They began to "get their act together." Instead of looking back toward Egypt, they began looking forward. Today's text is the last in a sequence of upbeat, positive, faith-filled events. The appointment of the overseers who would actually assign the land to each tribe and family was the exclamation point (today's text). What had been a vision that only the faithful could see was going to be fact. The promised land was going to be more than an idea; it was going to be a deed, a plot, a place. . . my place. What God had started in Exodus 3 was coming down to the wire. I found Numbers 21:10 through chapter 34 heartening. This text is a little bit like the birth of Jesus. People looked forward for so long for the birth of the Messiah. . . and then it actually happened.

Little children born in Egypt made the trip across the Red Sea, stood beside frightened parents at Sinai, saw Moses occasionally. . . soon those kids forgot about Egypt. The wilderness was the only home they had ever known. Going back to Egypt had no attraction for them; going on to the promised land became the dream. This text is from that period of time when they were so close to the promised land they could almost taste it.

I've tried to imagine their state of mind. They were different from their parents. The wilderness had something to do with it, but the text tells us there was a better reason they were different from their cowering, complaining parents—God had been at work. God had taken the children of slaves and made a useful tool. The mission born at Sinai was nearing completion. Let's look at what became of the children who grew up in the wilderness under Moses. . . and God. In some ways it is almost a blueprint for modern churches. Listen up!

The End of Looking Back—They Began to Believe

A common theme of the older generation was the appeal to return to Egypt: "The Israelites groaned under their slavery and cried out. Out of the slavery their cry for help rose up to God. God heard their groaning and. . . God took notice of them" (Ex 2:23-25). They had forgotten the toil and oppression, the brutality and hopelessness of Egypt. Now the rigors of the wilderness made Egypt look good to them.

Three times in chapters 11–20 appeals are made to return to Egypt.
- "Now when the people complained, 'If only we had meat to eat! We remember the fish we used to eat in Egypt for nothing, the cucumbers, the melons, the leeks, the onions, and the garlic' " (11:1-6). Egypt was looking good.
- After the negative report of the spies, "All the congregation raised a loud cry. . . . 'Would that we had died in the land of Egypt!. . . Would it not be better for us to go back to Egypt?' " (14:1-4).
- And again, "Now there was no water.. . . The people quarreled with Moses and said, 'Would that we had died when our kindred died before the LORD. . . . Why have you brought us up out of Egypt, to bring us to this wretched place?' " (20:2-8).

The memory of Egypt was strong, and the longer the older generation stayed in the wilderness, the better Egypt looked. Misery and bondage in Egypt were forgotten; all they could see was present hardship.

The desert generation had no memory of Egypt. Memory can be a heavy load. The new generation did not look back; they looked forward. Their idea of progress was not going back to what was; it was fleshing out the dream of the promised land. They had faith that the dream could become reality.

The End of Losing—They Began to Obey

When the Israelites first came out of Egypt they were a pitiful bunch. They would invade the space of a tribe, and the tribe would fight them. Usually Israel would lose. I think this pattern of losing had something to do with the way the ten negative spies saw Canaan. The idea that God would fight for them made Caleb and Joshua give a different report. The ten negative spies could not see God or victory.

Defeat is contagious. One defeat opens the door to the next: "We are not able to go up against this people, for they are stronger than we" (13:31b). Not only did they lose the last battle; in their heads they had already lost the next one. Such was the state of mind of ex-slaves. For a time they were glad to be out of Egypt and free, but the prospect of going forward to a land of their own was more than they could envision.

The young people in the wilderness came to two wonderful ideas:
• We are strong. We can win.
• God fights for us. Let's obey God.

And so the new generation moved out. They had faith in God, and they obeyed God. They did not hang back; they did not run ahead. In step with God they defeated Sihon and the Amorites (21:21-32), King Og of Bashan (21:33-35), and the Midianites (31:1-12). It was bloody work. There is nothing in it like Jesus and the Sermon on the Mount, but the author believed this was necessary for God's people to have a home. The new generation acted in concert with God; obedience and victory were joined. God fought their battles.

I don't think God held the older generation of Israelites in contempt. God was not *for* the younger and *against* the older generation. It was the "let's go back to Egypt" and "we can't do it" that God despised. And so God waited until the faithless generation slipped away. . . and then God moved. Congregations still have to wait for negative, faithless people to step offstage. The older generation did not change God's ultimate goal; they did change God's timetable. God got Israel to Canaan; it just took longer than intended. That's church work.

The End of Moses—They Began to Build a Nation

I find Numbers 27:12-23 sad. Moses had done so much right. He had risked himself. He had led when no one else was able or willing. But it was not for Moses to take Israel to the promised land. His job was to get them through the wilderness; someone else would lead from there. The Lord's choice to succeed Moses was Joshua: "Take Joshua son of Nun, a man in whom is the spirit, and lay your hand upon him" (27:18). Aaron, Moses' brother and the high priest, was dead. Now Joshua was replacing Moses.

It was a "changing of the guard." The old order gave way to the new. Moses was allowed to "go up this mountain of the Abarim range, and see the land that I have given to the Israelites. When you have seen it, you also shall be gathered to your people, as your brother Aaron was" (27:12-13). A fuller account of the death of Moses is given in Deuteronomy 23. It was on top of Mt. Nebo that Moses viewed the promised land, and then he just never came down from the mountain. The giant in Israel was gone: "Never since has there arisen a prophet in Israel like Moses, whom the LORD knew face to face. He was unequaled for all the signs and wonders that the LORD sent him to perform" (Deut 34:10-11).

What now? Israel had to learn to live without and beyond Moses. No one would argue that Eleazar was Aaron, but he was a good man. Joshua was no Moses, but he had the spirit of the Lord in him. He was willing, and at Jericho he got the job done.

The setting for Numbers 34 is late wilderness, almost on the eve of entrance into Canaan. They had to fight their way in. Joshua knew how to do that. Joshua and Eleazar presided over the division of the promised land. One man from each of the nine-and-a-half tribes (ten men) was chosen to work under the direction of Joshua and Eleazar (34:16-29). Imagine the pressure brought to bear on those people!

Israel is a small land, and there is considerable variety of terrain. Who gets the good land? Who will be given scruffy places? How can you do this job and keep the peace? God foresaw all my questions. Before they ever entered Canaan, a committee was in place to sort through the devilish details.

God was looking beyond Moses. There had to be new leadership. If God could get Israel beyond Moses, a congregation can find a successor to the best preacher. Usually the question is put poorly. We ask, "Can anyone follow our Moses?" Actually someone can. . . if we will let the new leader lead. When Israel was spoon-fed by Moses, they were a collection of people. When they began to create a new leadership, they were on their way to becoming a nation.

The End of Wilderness—They Would Have to Change

The generation that came out of Egypt had to adapt to wandering and wilderness. Their children grew up in the wilderness; it was wild and filled with adventure. Moses was larger than life, and God was as near as the "tent of meeting." They saw the cloud and smoke at Sinai when God made covenant. They saw Moses when he came down the mountain with the Ten Commandments. That's exciting stuff.

But our text anticipates another change. Can these people who have wandered for forty years settle down and make a nation? Can they live after Moses when God is not so obvious? Can they make homes, dig wells, plow ground, stay put? Our text is about the day when all that was dreamed became fact, deed, tract, dirt, place! I've seen people go through graduate school dreaming of being a doctor, a lawyer, a pastor. The dream comes to pass. But the real is not nearly as exciting as the dream. Often, making a solid law practice is not nearly as exciting as imagining one.

Israel did not find life in Canaan a picnic. Read Joshua and Judges to get the picture. The faith that was so strong when they entered Canaan slipped. The gods of the Canaanites teased and pulled at them. They flirted with idolatry for hundreds of years. The real was not ideal. What do you do with life when reality gives your dream a jolt? Wilderness called for heroic faith; Canaan required maintenance faith. There is a huge difference. Could Israel change and settle down? Can we?

Notes

Notes

nextsunday
STUDIES

1 Peter
Keep Hope Alive

This study of First Peter focuses on keeping hope alive in the face of pressures and circumstances that could possibly extinguish it completely, or worse, turn authentic faith into a pale replica of the real thing.

Apocalyptic Literature

This study examines five apocalyptic texts in the Bible—from Zechariah, Daniel, Matthew, and Revelation. With each new year bringing a new prediction of impending doom, it is always a perfect time to get the story straight. Apocalyptic literature does not address the future. It addresses our present.

Approaching a Missional Mindset

The World isn't the same as it once was. We must be the church in a new place, in unimagined ways, and with a wider range of people. Engage your small group with the radical and refreshing challenge of developing a "missional lifestyle."

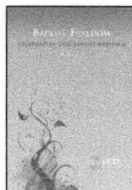

Baptist Freedom
Celebrating Our Baptist Heritage

What makes a Baptist a Baptist? Of course, the ultimate answer is simple: membership in a local Baptist church. But there are all kinds of Baptist churches! What are the spiritual and theological marks of a Baptist? What is the shape and the feel of Baptist Christianity?

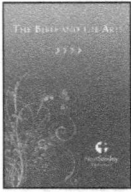

The Bible and the Arts

God has used artistic expression throughout the centuries to convey truth, offer blessing, and urge believers to deeper faithfulness. In modern life, artistic expression flourishes, from movies to books to music to paintings to photographs. Sometimes artists are intentional about trying to portray God's truths. Other times, perhaps God is working even when the artist is unaware of it. As believers, we may hear and see God at work in many art forms.

Challenges of the Christian Life

The way of the cross is difficult, and taking Jesus seriously means looking honestly at how we fall short of God's best hopes for us and seeing how much we need God's grace. For all of us there are times when we need to remember that Christ is our saving grace and recommit ourselves to the journey of faith, rediscovering, again and again, the life-giving purpose described in the book of Ephesians.

Christ Is Born!

Even in the midst of difficult circumstances, Advent is a time when we can find hope. Much like today, people in the 1st century church faced struggles. Examining the Gospel of Matthew, lessons include "Waiting for Christ," "Preparing for Christ," "Expecting Christ," "Announcing Christ," and "The Arrival of Christ."

Christians and Hunger

These sessions challenge us to apply gospel lenses and holy imagination to what literally gives us energy to live: food. With God's grace, we have the opportunity to imagine communities where tables are large and all are fed.

Christmas in Mark

In the early chapters of Mark, we will encounter a Christmas story. This story, however, will not be quite like the one told by other Gospel writers, but it will resonate with the reality of your life. Mark doesn't deny the beauty or reality of the nativity; however, he seems to believe that Christmas begins—the gospel begins—when Christ intrudes upon the hard realities of life.

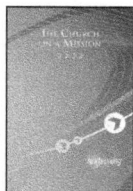

The Church on a Mission

What does it mean to be a church on a mission? The lesson of Acts 1:8 is that we must simultaneously carry out Christ's mandate at home, in our region, in places that have been our blind spots, and around the world.

Colossians
Living the Faith Faithfully

Paul's letter to the Colossians begins with a high-minded philosophical defense of the faith, but concludes with a collection of extremely practical advice for living by faith. This study addresses the questions many Christians face today, helping them apply Paul's practical advice in their own lives.

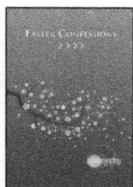

Easter Confessions

Easter confession is often found on many different lips in the Gospel of John. When we listen carefully, those ancient confessions still echo into this new millennium.

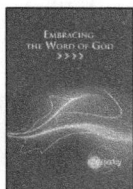

Embracing the Word of God

We live during a time of transition in Christian history. Basic assumptions about the truth of the Christian faith are being questioned, not only by nonbelievers, but by Christians themselves. First John offers a starting point for understanding of what it means to "be" Christian.

Esther: A Woman of Discretion and Valor

The book of Esther is not a record of historical facts as such. Rather, it is a magnificent narrative that refuses to interpret life as being driven by coincidence or happenstance. In the otherwise unknown characters of Esther, Haman, and Mordecai, we trace the movement of the divine hand as God collaborates with God's risk-taking people to rescue them from the hand of their enemies.

Facing Life's Challenges

This study explores four significant challenges common to most persons of faith: the challenge of new light, the challenge of time's limit, the challenge of living with mystery, and the challenge of authentic spirituality. Although these issues are neither simple nor easy to ponder, this study effectively leads us in confronting these challenges.

Galatians
Freedom in Christ
Paul wrote with fiery passion, as you will notice from the opening paragraphs of this letter to the Galatians. But his language reveals that he was writing about a crucially important issue—the very nature of salvation in Christ.

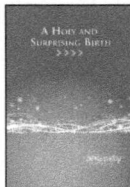

A Holy and Surprising Birth
Christmas begins here—discover these five love stories from the book of Luke and renew your appreciation of God's laborious effort to birth our salvation.

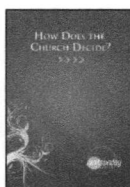

How Does the Church Decide?
An array of decisions draw energy and time from church members. These decisions may be theological, such as mode of baptism, aesthetic, such as the color of the sanctuary carpet, or functional, such as the selection of a new minister. This study will consider how the church has made its decisions in the past to help guide our decisions today.

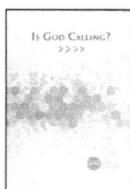

Is God Calling?
Witness the varying forms of God's call, the variety of people called, and the variety of responses. Perhaps God's call to you will become clearer.

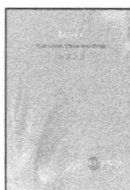

James
Gaining True Wisdom
If we'll be honest with God and ourselves as we study what James says, we can make great strides toward wisdom and a living faith.

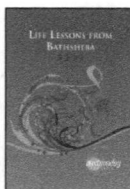

Life Lessons from Bathsheba
Who was Bathsheba? She was a complex figure who developed from the silent object of David's lust into a powerful, vocal, and influential queen mother.

Life Lessons from David

In the Bible, we catch David in the various stages of the human journey: childhood, adolescence, adulthood, and senior adulthood. From the biblical treatment of the stages of David's life, we can land some insights to assist us in better understanding the human journey.

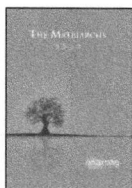

The Matriarchs

The matriarchs of Genesis offer their lives as a testimony of faith, perseverance, and audacity. We learn from their mistakes and suffering. We will gain the hope of Hagar, the joy of Sarah, and the audacity of Rebekah as we are challenged to examine our prejudices and our insecurities while studying Esau and Jacob's wives.

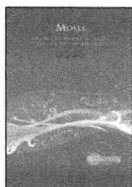

Moses
From the Burning Bush to the Promised Land

We would do well to trace the life of Moses so we might discover how his life changed, both personally and as Israel's leader, as he learned what it meant to love God with all his heart, soul, and strength.

Old Testament Promises to God

Some individuals may feel that our promises couldn't possibly mean anything to God. Perhaps the real question is this: under what circumstances should or do we make such promises? The Old Testament contains several examples of people making promises to God, using the unique form of a biblical "vow."

The Passion of Christ

The four lessons in this unit highlight the faith struggles of the early disciples. In lesson one, Jesus addresses the issues of faith and practice. In lesson two, we meet Judas who, like us, struggled with God's Kingdom and human kingdoms. In lesson three, the issue of temptation reminds us that our faith journey is a constant challenge. Lesson Four invites us to remember Peter's experience of "faith failure." Peter's failure, however, is not the final word. There is forgiveness.

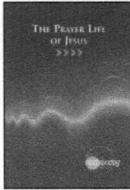

The Prayer Life of Jesus

The study of Jesus' prayer life can deepen our own prayer practices. These five sessions examine the importance of prayer at various stages of Jesus' life and ministry. He made no important decisions without consulting God.

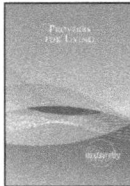

Proverbs for Living

Long ago, a collection of wise teachers committed themselves to the ways of God and collected this wisdom into what we know as the book of Proverbs. These four lessons explore the simple truth of Proverbs: there is a good life to be had—a life lived in faithfulness to God.

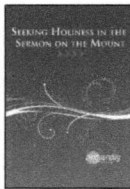

Seeking Holiness in the Sermon on the Mount

The Sermon on the Mount has long been recognized as the pinnacle of Jesus' teaching. But with this importance in mind, it's easy to think of Jesus' teachings as lofty and idealistic, offering little guidance for everyday life. Perhaps Jesus' sermon allows us to see beyond ourselves, beyond our own failures and shortcomings—revealing God's intention for our lives.

Spiritual Disciplines
Obligation or Opportunity?

The spiritual disciplines help deepen a believer's faith and increases his or her intimacy with Christ. In this study, we take a deeper look at some of the disciplines and consider their practice as a response to God's love.

Stewardship
A Way of Living

Great News! Stewardship is not about money! At least not *just* about money. Certainly, stewardship relates to money, and, yes, we need to tithe. However, stewardship branches out into multiple areas of life. Properly practiced, this act of service can lead to peace and purpose in living.

The Ten Commandments

When the Ten Commandments are in the news, it is usually because a judge or teacher has hung them up on the walls. The Ten Commandments do not need to be posted or even preached nearly so much as they need to be practiced and viewed as life-giving, joyful affirmations of a better way of life.

What Would Jesus Say?
A Lenten Study

To address what Jesus would say, we need to discover what Jesus did say. These lessons will attempt to help us understand Jesus' teachings and apply them today.

**NextSunday Studies
are available from**

NextSunday
Resources

www.ingramcontent.com/pod-product-compliance
Lightning Source LLC
Chambersburg PA
CBHW070552030426
42337CB00016B/2462